Fifty Hikes in Vermont

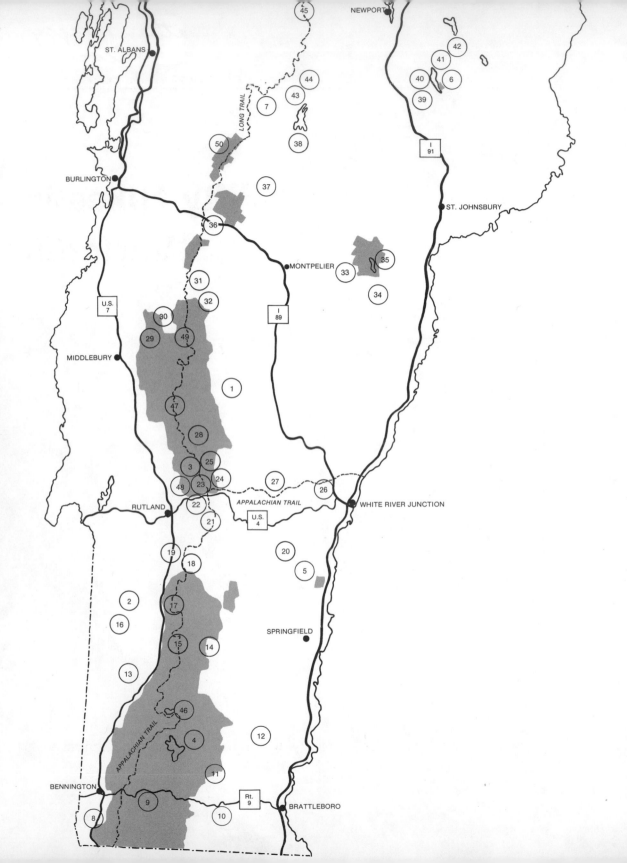

Ruth and Paul Sadlier

Fifty Hikes in Vermont

**Walks, Day Hikes, and Backpacking Trips
in the Green Mountain State**

with Photographs by the Authors

**New Hampshire Publishing Company
Somersworth**

Thank you, John

First printing: 1974

Second printing: 1976

Published by the New Hampshire Publishing Company,
15 Interstate Drive, Somersworth, N.H. 03878

Library of Congress catalog card number: 73-90338
SBN: 0-912274-38-7

Manufactured in the United States of America

Maps by Pat Mathewson

Contents

With increasing amounts of leisure time, people are turning more to healthy outdoor activities. Hiking and backpacking offer myriad opportunities to gain relief from the complexities and luxuries of our modern world.

What we might term the "appeal of the wilds" draws us out into the clean, invigorating air of scenic woodlands and towering mountains. And yet—there is more to it than just walking along a trail or looking at a view. We gain an appreciation for nature's unique values: simplicity, silence, and solitude. We learn that we must depend more upon ourselves than on external aids. We learn that by "roughing it" we can better appreciate what we have. In the end—we learn more about ourselves.

The Fifty Hikes

The trips in this book span the entire state of Vermont and include its five highest peaks (all over 4,000 feet). Twenty of the excursions are situated on the well-known Long Trail which

The authors on Mount Abraham

extends 262 miles from the Massachusetts to the Canadian border. The other thirty follow the theme of (Vermont Poet Laureate) Robert Frost's poem "The Road Not Taken." They introduce you to some of the "less traveled" peaks and areas.

We selected hikes in all sections of the state, for both the inexperienced and experienced hiker. To help you determine appropriate ones, we've included classification criteria at the beginning of each trek. They are:

Class I:
Mostly flat-to-gradual grade; no obstacles.

Class II:
Mostly gradual-to-moderate grade with possible isolated steep sections; little, if any, ledge climbing.

Class III:
Gradual-to mostly-moderate grade with occasional steep sections; minimal ledge climbing, possibly requiring use of hands.

Class IV:
Moderate-to-steep grade; much ledge climbing; use of hands necessary.

Class V:
Mostly steep grade; extensive

ledge climbing; much use of hands required.

Forty-five of the hikes are day trips. Five offer chances for more extended, backpacking journeys. Of these, two can be handled on a regular weekend (two days/ one night); two, on a long weekend (three days/two nights); and one, in a week (five days/four nights). In addition, the Presidential Range (Hike 49) and Middlebury Gap to Brandon Gap (Hike 47) trips can be combined to form a second five day/four night outing.

You will also find frequent mileage checks—via landmarks—in each hike. These will keep you informed on how far you've gone— or have to go—without requiring use of a pedometer.

When consulting the sketch map for each hike, note that the top always represents North. All of the trails follow well-marked or easily-recognized routes.

Elevation, Vertical Rise, Distance, Hiking Time

These categories (plus "Class," described above) appear at the beginning of each hike and give you a capsule projection of what lies ahead.

The elevations are those appearing on U.S. Geological Survey (U.S.G.S.) maps and posted signs atop summits. However, if you climb a 4,000-foot mountain it does not mean you've risen 4,000 feet upon reaching the top. You must subtract the height of your starting point from the mountain's height to determine the actual rise in elevation. Vertical rise provides this information. Sometimes you will climb up and down valleys before ascending to a summit. Those preliminary upward climbs are included in the vertical rise figure. In short, we are using "vertical rise" to indicate the total amount of *upward* climbing entailed in a hike. As a general rule, you can expect that, the greater the vertical rise per mile, the more strenuous the hike.

Distance gives the exact mileage from start to finish. Almost all the hikes return you to your starting point via a loop—or perhaps the same—trail. Exceptions are three of the overnights (Coolidge Range, Presidential Range and Middlebury Gap to Brandon Gap) which start at one point and finish miles away, thereby necessitating additional transportation plans.

Don't be surprised to find some mileage differences between those listed in this book and the same ones appearing on trail signs erected by the Green Mountain Club and the U.S. Forest Service. For example, the East Branch Trail to Somerset Reservoir: we measured it at 4.7 miles one way, but read on the Forest Service sign that it was 6.5 miles, and in the club's literature that it was 5.5 miles! We will not try to argue that our distances are the only true ones, although we do believe they are accurate. We will, however, state that our hiking times were computed with care. We suggest you depend upon them whenever a difference in mileage occurs. Remember that the hiking time means just that; it does not include rest, lunch, or observation stops. After a couple of hikes you should know how your pace compares with our steady-but-leisurely one and be able to apply this knowledge to other hikes.

The Mountains

While touring the lake that now bears his name, on July 4, 1609, Samuel Champlain made the first recorded mention of the Green Mountains. Of all the mountains in the world, they are among the oldest (close to four hundred million years old). They once rivaled the heights of such young peaks as Mount McKinley and Mount Rainier.

The bedrock which makes up most of the Green Mountain range was formed beneath the ocean, eons ago—of sea shells, shale, sand, and sedimentary clay. The hot, molten interior of the earth caused great upheavals in the ocean floor, pushing the sea back and giving birth to the mountains—which reared their heads to cool slowly. Fragmentation and additional eruptions in the earth's surface gave rise to other new peaks.

The Ice Age brought glaciers. Organic life was crushed beneath these frozen mile-thick masses. During Ice Age "summers," rivers coursed across the face of glaciers and ferried quantities of rocks to southern New England and Long Island Sound. Farmers have been plowing these glacial deposits out of fields and piling them into stone walls for hundreds of years.

Mountains were molded and carved by the thousands of years of glacial advancement and recession. Vermont's mountains of today have approximately the same elevation and contours as they did at the time of the final recession of the glaciers.

When only Indians inhabited America, Vermont was a virtual wilderness. Early settlers appeared and began to cut trees to clear land for cattle, corn, towns, and industries. They also reduced vast numbers of trees to cinders to obtain potash, which was in high demand for English industries. Logging empires of the 1800s ruthlessly slaughtered the virgin forests and exported the lumber to build new towns and cities along the Atlantic coast.

There were continual murmurings from conservationists about the large-scale pillaging of woodlands. In 1891 Joseph Battell confronted the Vermont Legislature and pleaded for protection of the wildlands. This "forestry movement" led to the founding of the Forest Association.

In 1912 the duties of this association were extended. State-owned model forests demonstrated the advantages of scientific cutting and planting to private woodlot owners. Forest management for both conservation and commerce came under this single authority. Lumbermen realized that it was good business to replace trees and perhaps increase their numbers, for future harvests.

Vermonters and the numbers of yearly visitors to the state can have an effect on the future history of the mountains and woodlands by continued concern and efforts for conservation.

Summit Houses

By the 1850s paths had been trodden to most of the highest peaks in Vermont. To accommodate the lucrative city tourist trade, carriage roads were built. Equinox Mountain, Mount Ascutney, Camel's Hump, Mount Mansfield, Lincoln Mountain, and Snake Mountain all offered bed and board in their summit houses. Sunsets, sunrises, hiking, dancing, and entertainment occupied the guests. Most of the summit houses were eventually lost to declines in business, fires . . . or porcupines.

Physical Fitness

Hiking demands proper conditioning. The best equipment will not help you reach your goal if you are out of shape. Once on the trail and beyond the limits of civilization you must depend upon your feet, legs, back, hands, and cardio-vascular system. A fit body will insure both enjoyment and completion of your trip.

This is not to say that most people should be fearful of attempting the hikes in Classes I and II, or even many of those in Class III. If time is not a factor and you can "go at your own pace" (which we recommend) you should find all of these within your reach. A few of the Class III hikes—plus those in Classes IV and V– are quite strenuous, though. These should not be attempted by anyone who does not exercise regularly (active, sinewy youth may be the exception here).

We believe that jogging provides the best all-around preparation for hiking. It strengthens not only the seventy-five percent of the body's muscles located in the lower back and below, but the heart and lungs as well. If extensive hiking is your objective, include some hills in your jog-

Beaver lodge

ging. If you cannot jog, walking is an alternate—though less effective—preparatory exercise.

Seasonal Hiking

The Vermont hiking season is limited only by your preference and ability. Although we personally are apt to go anytime, fall and winter are our favorites. When the leaves start to turn you are treated to one of nature's wonders. Cool air and rainbowed colors combine to give you a "natural high." Few regions of the world possess the large tracts of broad-leaved trees and favorable weather conditions that produce the vivid fall colors we enjoy in Vermont. As the air gets crisper and leaves tumble, light snow blankets the trails. Not deep enough to be a hindrance, this covering is dotted with animal tracks which unfold like a story book as you walk along. Heavy snows mean it's time to break out the snowshoes. (We don't suggest that novices begin their hiking in winter.)

Spring brings sprouting greens and lingering reminders of winter. Remember that snow may remain at higher elevations into May. Trails may be cluttered by trees and branches, and rutted in spots. June and July offer plenty of sunny days—and bugs. Take along plenty of insect repellent. If you like the feel of sweat dropping off your brow and dampening the small of your back, July and August are the months for you. September sees the end of bugs, still, warm days, and clear skies.

Rules and Regulations

You do not leave these behind when departing from civilization. Most rules and regulations have been developed to help us preserve woodlands and the wildlife living therein. Philosophies such as "leave nothing but footprints" carry important messages, but are not specific enough to check the careless rush of mankind.

Fire represents the greatest danger to our forests. The State of Vermont, accordingly, has laid down careful rules. Portable burners are classified as open fires from April 1 to November 1. A campfire permit is required for all fires outside developed areas, regardless of the type of fuel used. Local fire wardens or district forest rangers can supply these permits. Fires may be built in authorized fireplaces on state land and at shelters within the Green Mountain National Forest. Building fires on private property without the owner's consent is prohibited by state law from April 1 to November 1 (existence of a shelter, though, indicates that consent has been given for use of the stove or fireplace therein).

Fees are collected for use of state park facilities and Long Trail lodges. Large groups should carry tents when planning to stay overnight at a lodge or shelter—in order to prevent the overcrowding their sizeable numbers might cause.

Clothing and Equipment

Comfortable clothing for hiking is made of materials that allow a balance between ventilation and insulation. Insulation must prevent the loss of body heat. Ventilation is necessary to dissipate the water vapor released from the pores of the skin.

Fit is important. Legs must be able to move, bend, and stretch freely with no binding or chafing. Arm movement, too, must be unrestricted. Shorts that are roomy around the thighs are by far our favorites for warm weather. A day hike up a mountain requires packing longer pants because of unpredictable temperature changes at higher elevations. Wide-legged, lightweight rainpants are both warm and dry, and pull on easily over boots.

Cotton T-shirts breathe well, are lightweight, and feel good next to the skin (fishnet T-shirts are very popular too). Cotton chamois shirts provide good button-over warmth and, at 16 ounces, are a weight bargain. The hooded parka from a rainsuit can serve as either wetgear or windbreaker. We bring along featherweight rainsuits even on the sunniest days.

The cold and snow which can occur in the Vermont mountains from late fall through late spring demand specially designed clothing. Garments which provide maximum warmth at minimum weight are vital for survival and comfort when hiking in cold, windy conditions.

Boots are your most important purchase. Carefully chosen footwear can cushion the foot over rough terrain, protect ankles from twisting and spraining, and provide a reasonable degree of warmth and water repellency. City footwear is generally useless, even potentially dangerous. For all the aforementioned reasons, we recommend hiking boots. Medium weight ones (three pounds) are suited to the fifty hikes described in this book. Lug soles are durable, flexible, and grip well. Boot uppers and seams need to be treated with an oil, grease, wax, or silicone. Socks provide insulation, help to cushion the feet, and absorb perspiration and friction between boot and foot. A heavy wool sock fitted over a lighter, inner wool one is a comfortable and practical combination. Wool, even if it gets wet, will keep your feet warm.

Due to serious conservation concerns, the romantic blazing woodfire must become a thing of the past. Downed wood is an increasingly scarce commodity and fire presents a constant danger to woodlands and wildlife. A variety of gas-fueled, compact stoves are easily available, and preferable for the use of hikers.

Tents can provide shelter from rain, wind, snow, and insects. They come in a wide range of prices and styles. The choice should be based on your own numbers and needs. Weight and simplicity of design should be of paramount concern. Our three-pound, nylon backpacking tent can be erected with relative ease and speed, thanks to its one-piece, attached-rainfly construction.

Down sleeping bags are to be recommended for their light weight, low bulk, and excellent insulating properties. A foam pad can supply protection from ground cold and moisture as well as provide sleeping comfort.

Packs and frames should be chosen with care. Good frames come in several sizes and are s-shaped, to conform to body contours. With the addition of a full hip belt and water-proof (as distinguished from water-repellent) packbag, you will be well-equipped.

First Aid and Survival

The best medicine is prevention. Become familiar with what lies ahead, bring suitable supplies, and know what to do in an emergency.

Traveling alone can be the greatest potential danger to hikers. We encountered many enthusiastic climbers who had either started on their own or had a companion leave somewhere along the way. With no one available to assist in case of accident the chances of dangerous complications are greater.

Brush up on first aid procedures and bring a first aid kit with you. Have a compass and map (U.S.G.S. maps give excellent details of an area—even though some were made twenty years ago) and know how to use them. (In Vermont the compass points about fifteen degrees west of true North.) Take a flashlight and extra batteries— just in case. If you do become lost or injured—don't panic. Remain calm, assess your situation, and act according to your knowledge of the area.

Food

Whether you plan a day hike or backpacking trip, remember to keep your food light. Cans add both weight and bulk. Fresh foods might spoil or melt.

Many companies produce large varieties of freeze-dried foods which are ideal for today's hiker. Light in weight and surprisingly tasty, they are a convenience for the day hiker and a salvation for

the backpacker. Whatever your tastes, you can satisfy them with freeze-dried meats, eggs, vegetables, soups, desserts, or fruits. Many of these foods are ready to eat after adding water (either cold or hot) and eliminate the need to spend hours preparing meals. Their packages can also be easily tucked into a litter bag for the return trip.

For an energy treat you might consider cheese, rather than chocolate. Cheeses have a high energy output; the drier ones are best. Romano, Parmesan, Provolone, and Kasseri are the driest. Even relatively dry Swiss and Cheddar have a high water content. Most people do not realize that because of its high fat content (more than fifty percent in unsweetened varieties) chocolate is much harder to digest than other candy. Eating large amounts of it just before or during strenuous activity often produces an upset stomach, instead of a spurt of energy.

Flora and Fauna

Throughout this book we have passed on information which will aid in the identification of trees, shrubs, flowers, animals, and

birds you may see.

Animals and birds (and some insects) can often be recognized by their "sign." Such signs include tracks, droppings, nests, burrows, dams, gnawings, rubbings, and scratchings. To the careful observer, they can indicate an animal's search for food, a battle, a slow or fast passage, perhaps even its age.

Signs are all you will see of most animals in the areas of the fifty hikes. Black bears and bobcats go out of their way to avoid humans. You shouldn't encounter any dangerous snakes. Raccoons, skunks, foxes, opossums, owls, and bats are nocturnal animals.

Songbirds, squirrels, and chipmunks will flutter and scamper close, to look you over. If you're very quiet and patient, you may be fortunate enough to see a beaver or muskrat at one of the active ponds. Early in the morning or at dusk a deer may come to a lakeside to drink. Partridge will startle you with their blurry takeoffs. Hawks ride effortlessly on the air currents near the summits of many peaks. Porcupines display unique eccentricities. They love salt and will happily demolish a pair of boots, or perhaps a pack—if such are left within their reach overnight.

Leaves, bark, flowers, fruit, buds, fragrance, color, and dimensions are clues used in the identification of trees, shrubs, and flowers. You are encouraged to help protect the forest and alpine vegetation by leaving all plant life as you found it.

Preserving Our Heritage

Some guidelines for insuring that what we enjoy today will be there for others to enjoy tomorrow:

Keep your group small.
Stay only a short time in one place.
Leave campsites cleaner than you found them.
Carry out empty what you carried in full.
Pick up the litter of less thoughtful persons.
Don't contaminate water.
Bury body waste.
Burn burnables only if a fire is permitted.
Do not cut trees or branches.
Leave no sign of your presence.

SOME ADDRESSES TO KNOW ABOUT:

Forest Supervisor
Green Mountain National Forest
151 West St.
Rutland, Vermont 05701

Green Mountain Club
P.O. Box 94
Rutland, Vermont 05701

State of Vermont
Department of Forests and Parks
Montpelier, Vermont 05602

United States Geological Survey
Washington, D.C. 20242

Introductory Hikes

The 240,000-acre Green Mountain National Forest offers a wide variety of natural attractions. This showcase of preserved land stretches nearly two thirds the length of Vermont.

A trip through the forest is not just a hike in the woods but rather an excursion into Vermont itself. Rolling countryside, small towns, and slackening pace typify the simpler, quieter way of life that is Vermont.

A leisurely walk through the Texas Falls Recreation Area near Hancock will introduce you to the state's natural endowments. The Hancock Branch pours its waters through an awesome descending gorge, in a unique display of nature's magnitude. Explanatory guideposts along the trail help you better understand the forest's ways and the need for its careful management in today's technological world.

On the Robert Frost Memorial Drive (Vt. 125) go east 12.9 miles from Middlebury, or west 3.0 miles from Hancock. Turn north onto the road for the Texas Falls National Forest Recreation Area. After .5 miles you will reach a parking area on the left

Texas Falls

Texas Falls Nature Trails

1. Texas Falls Nature Trail

Class: I

Distance (along the trail): 1 mile
Hiking time: as long as you want

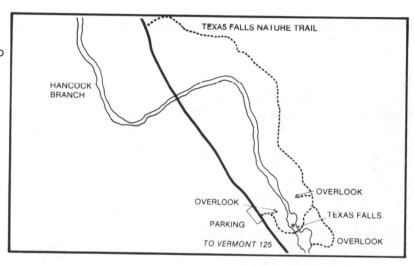

and a sign indicating the Nature Trail on the right.

A path leads down from the road to an attractive setting. A combination wood and stone fence guides you along the trail. You see below a deep gorge with water rushing through. It begins up to the left in a flat pool and gushes down into a white, frothy basin. Slithering over smooth ledge, it winds and spills its way to quieter pools below. Towering hemlocks help focus your view upon the surging water.

Wind your way up more man-made, stone steps to the signed intersection. A right turn leads you along a spur trail and an overlook high above the gorge. The pounding water sound fills your ears as you look the length of the gorge and see several water-falls, one atop the other.

Return to the intersection and begin the interpretive section of the trail. Almost immediately you come to post # 1. The dying and decaying trees of the forest help to enrich the soil around them with new organic material. Leaves and other natural materials fall to the ground and decay, adding more vital nutrients to the soil. At this station you will observe logs undergoing the process of decay.

Opposite station #1 is another spur to an overlook. Log benches offer a chance to just sit and linger in this peaceful setting. From here you can see the upper section of the falls.

The flat, spongy trail leads on to station #2. The source of the Hancock Branch stream is a forested watershed. Because of the overhead branches and foliage of the trees and the carpet of leaves on the forest floor protecting the soil from rain erosion, the stream remains unmuddied.

Passing a log bench, the trail reaches stations #3 and #4. Behind station #3 are low plants known as witch hobble. They are a favorite food of deer. Look closely to see if any of their tops have been nibbled.

Station #4 marks the location of a massive boulder. Through the process of symbiosis, a plant community thrives on top of this great rock. Its greenish-grey, crust-like growth is a type of lichen and is composed of two distinctly different plants. Water is collected by the sponge-like fungus. The alga uses this water in photosynthesis and produces food for both itself and the fungus. Thus, these two plants are mutually interdependent; neither could live alone on the rock's surface.

Texas Falls Nature Trail

As you begin a gradual climb, the hillside rises steeply to the right. The trail continues to parallel the river as it drops down to the left. Scattered openings in the trees enable you to glimpse the rushing stream.

Approaching station #5 you can see where the river courses beneath the road bridge. This station identifies a sugar maple. This is the tree from which the famous Vermont maple syrup comes. To be fit for tapping, a tree must be at least forty years old, about sixty feet high and one foot in diameter. A grove of these prime sap producers is called a sugarbush. The first March thaw is the time when new tap holes are drilled. Buckets are hung on the sap spouts and checked several times a week through March and into April. It takes about forty-five gallons of boiled-down sap to produce a gallon of pure maple syrup.

The trail begins a slight descent as it approaches signpost #6. Here a large hemlock rises above you. These trees may grow to eighty feet in height and three feet in diameter. They feature irregularly arranged, half-inch-long needles, backed by twin silvery lines on the underside.

Unlike balsam, hemlock needles are not fragrant when crushed. The hemlock is a part of the diet of a variety of wildlife. Porcupines chew on the bark and the seeds are eaten by squirrels and birds.

Station #7, just ahead on the left, displays a botanical oddity. Maple trees normally have a single stem and root system. The maple near the post has one root system supporting a number of stems. This is the result of the breaking of the original stem. The hardiest sprouts formed by the dormant buds at the root collar survived, forming this mass.

Just before a bend in the trail you reach signpost #8. The rows of small holes girdling this hemlock were dug by a yellow-bellied sapsucker. This woodpecker digs out holes and eats the inner bark. During this process sap oozes from the indentations. The sapsucker returns later to feast upon any insects attracted to the sap.

After this last station, the path drops down to the road. Why not reverse your route and enjoy it all once again? With ample time to picnic and relax you have all the ingredients for a perfect day.

Texas Falls Nature Trail

2. Merck Forest Nature Trail

Class: I
Vertical rise: 400 feet
Distance (around loop): 1 mile
Hiking time: It's up to you

Merck Forest Nature Trail

The 2,600 acres of woodland, meadows, ponds, and streams which comprise the Merck Forest were donated by George W. Merck in 1950. He felt a close kinship to the land and believed that these meadows and woods represented the typical Vermont upland farms, then rapidly dying out as commercial ventures. He envisioned the coming takeover of Vermont's open lands by rapidly increasing numbers of outdoor enthusiasts, and realized the need to preserve extensive areas for public use. He also hoped that the Merck Forest could show how farms might be converted to multiple-use properties.

The Merck Forest is made up of several old, abandoned farms. Although much of the original grazing land has become forest (through both natural seeding and planting), some of the meadows are mowed to keep a balance between forest

Merck Forest Nature Trail

and open land. A year-round program of logging and reforestation maintains the forest's productivity. Resultant wildlife habitats provide suitable homes for a variety of animals. The forest also helps visitors become better acquainted with, and more understanding of, their environment.

This hike can be enjoyed by the entire family. Its relatively short length allows for leisurely walking and plenty of exploration.

Signboards at the seven stations along the trail offer detailed information about tree plantations, gardens, and wildlife habitats. You'll learn about fungi, soil and climatic conditions, control of animal populations, and forest life cycles. Signs will also introduce you to the following trees along the way: white birch, sugar maple, aspen, larch, black cherry, apple, and oak.

You'll reach the entrance to the Merck Forest on Vt. 315 by driving 3.3 miles east from the junction of Vt. 153 and 315 in Rupert, or 2.6 miles west from the junction of Vt. 30 and 315 in East Rupert. Turn south onto the Forest Road.

The road immediately forks to either side of the "Merck Forest Foundation, Inc." sign. Bear

right and drive ½ mile to the parking area. Walk to the information area near the gate. Register (for Merck Forest rules, see Hike 16), and take advantage of the pamphlets and the colorful wooden map displayed there.

The Nature Trail begins across the road from this information stand. Follow its moderate-to-steep climb past the first two stations and down a long slope to station #3. Go left onto the dirt road beyond this station, and follow it to the barn.

The barn is the center of the Merck Forest education program, offering exhibits which introduce you to the many plants and animals that

appear in the forest. Instruction in conservation education is made available. The qualified staff works efficiently to provide this—and other—helpful information.

The Nature Trail resumes at the big sign in the field below the barn. After crossing the field you come to a small fork near the gate to a pasture. Bear right onto the wider trail.

The trail descends gradually and flattens out as it passes stations #4 and #5. Well-shaded, and only moderately steep, it then swings right and continues to climb past the last two stations, back to the parking lot.

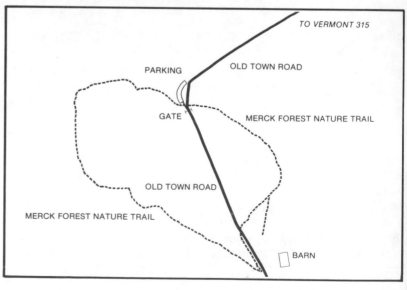

3. Pine Hill Park:
Forest Ecology Nature Trail

Class: I
Distance (around loop): 1 mile
Hiking time: up to you

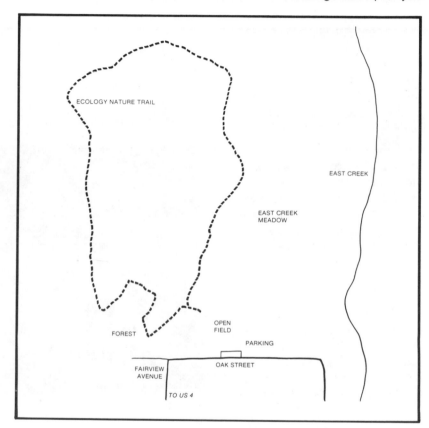

In 1761 Governor Benning Wentworth of New Hampshire chartered Rutland. The first grantee, John Murray of Rutland, Massachusetts, christened the new settlement. A prosperous gristmill and sawmill established in the 1770s made Rutland a flourishing frontier town within a few years.

After the Civil War, Colonel Redfield Proctor returned to Rutland and transformed its one-hundred-year-old marble business into a highly successful operation. Located in the western part of Rutland, its marble deposits were among the world's richest.

Today Rutland is a small American city, a busy center of retail trading and industrial activity. A section of the city has been preserved for natural recreational activities. Pine Hill Park sits quietly in Rutland's northwestern corner, away from the bustle of its shopping district and factories.

The Forest Ecology Nature Trail is one of a number of marked trails in the park. You may obtain guide pamphlets from the Rutland Recreation Department (on Court Street). Pale blue paint spots and numbered signposts keyed to the pamphlet mark the way.

To reach the park, drive west on U.S. 4 through Rutland. Shortly after crossing the cement bridge over East Creek, route 4 bears sharply left. Turn right here onto Pierpoint Avenue. At the end of Pierpoint, just beyond the Northwest School, continue straight onto Fairview Avenue. Turn right at the end of Fairview onto Oak Street.

Pine Hill Park appears quickly on your left. Park along the edge of the road.

The Forest Ecology Nature Trail begins at the left corner of the large East Creek meadow before you.

The guide pamphlet acquaints you with the animal, vegetable, and mineral residents of Pine Hill Park. It gives detailed information on how harmony is naturally maintained in the woodland community and helps you understand the important role we all must play in protecting the environment.

The area near station #5 has been cultivated with its wildlife in mind. The pruning and removal of some larger trees have allowed apple, black cherry, thornapple, and honeysuckle to thrive. The twigs, fruits, and seeds of these trees and shrubs provide food for animals and birds.

The large boulders near station #11 support a colony of mosses and lichens. The mosses form a furry green carpet on the boulders. Lichen are composed of two types of plants: a fungus and an alga. The spongelike fungus collects water which supplies the alga with minerals and water and keeps it from drying out. In return, the alga supplies food for both the fungus and itself through the process of photosynthesis.

Rotting stumps and fallen trees in the area of station #15 return nutrients to the surrounding soil through the process of decay Live plants and trees utilize these recycled nutrients for growth.

At station #24 there is a unique appeal to good forest manners. A permanent collection of litter is on display. (All litter should, of course, be disposed of properly.

The recommended solution—and the lesson to be learned from this display—is recycling.)

The Forest Ecology Trail terminates at the edge of East Creek Meadow, back near signpost #1.

Common garter snake

4. Somerset Reservoir

Class: II
Elevation: 2,100 feet
Vertical rise: 475 feet
Distance (round trip): 9.4 miles
Hiking time: 5 hours

If you want a full day of hiking, try this one. The East Branch Trail crosses suspension bridges, skirts beaver dams, and meanders undemandingly through a number of naturally varied areas. With the prospect of a picnic at the reservoir, this hike promises all the ingredients for a very satisfying day.

Note the distance and hiking time. You'll want to allow plenty of time for rest and observation stops and, also, for that picnic lunch. Don't get caught short of time or you may be forced to complete your hike in darkness.

From the intersection of Vt. 9 and Vt. 100 in Wilmington, go west on route 9. After 5.7 miles turn north at the green and white sign for Somerset. Follow this dirt road for 1.8 miles to the U.S. Forest Service sign for the East Branch Trail. Park along the widened side of the road.

The path drops down the embankment and crosses the Deerfield River via a long, bouncy suspension bridge. It turns right at a fork just ahead and makes its way up through a grassy open field.

Evergreens mix with the deciduous trees along the trail. Gentle

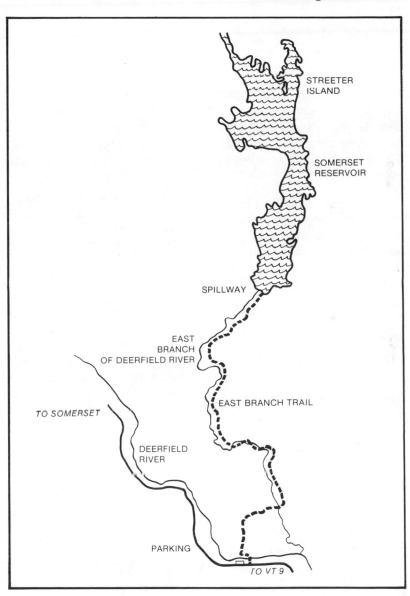

Somerset Reservoir

dips and rises characterize the way as it leads to another suspension bridge at .4 miles. This carries you across the East Branch of the Deerfield River.

Spruce and balsam needles cushion the path as it leads down evergreen lanes. The way is flat and the walking easy. Yellow birches alternate with conifers, as the trail varies from open to closed.

The river appears down to the left as the path crosses the first of several small streams. Logs and walkalongs help you across these waters. A good sense of balance can be helpful.

Beaver dams come into view on the left. Take time for a close inspection of the engineering involved in their construction. Sticks, branches, grass, dirt, and roots are all piled together to hold back the water. Once there is sufficient water to support a lodge and winter beaver activity, the dam is completed.

Note also the many gnawed tree stumps and wet meadowland filled with dead trees. Once a beaver pond, this area is in the process of becoming a meadow; and, eventually, a forest once again.

Swinging away from the river, the trail passes through a concentrated area of low spruces. It continues very flat and gradual and at 1.7 miles swings sharply right just before reaching the river.

The way parallels the water below a ridge line. It crosses a tributary at 1.9 miles and the river itself at 2.2 miles. For the next half mile the trail criss-crosses the water several times and travels parallel to it on both sides.

Leaving the river, the trail becomes rocky at times as it passes through extensive hardwood forests. Slender young trees predominate here. The ground is littered with older, dead trees in the process of decaying.

At 3.4 miles the trail approaches a large area of former beaver activity. Hundreds of barkless, sun-bleached logs lie strewn across the land. A deserted lodge can now be reached via dry land. It provides a good close-up of a beaver home.

After the beavers have created a pond, muskrats often move in to enjoy it. Mink, which love muskrat meat, are the next to arrive. Although the beavers have moved on, mink still live here. You may see their droppings along the East Branch Trail. Four to six inches long, these scats are blackish and irregularly segmented when they consist of fur. Fish remains make them rough, black, and glistening. Feathers and fowl meat cause smooth, light-colored scats.

The trail continues flat and smooth. Several brooks are crossed before it dips down through a large, grassy field. Rocks and roots fill the way as it parallels the river again.

Twisting and turning, the well-marked trail intersects with a road at 4.6 miles. Go right, and follow the winding road .1 miles up to the reservoir.

Filling the horizon at the far end of Somerset Reservoir is Stratton Mountain. Glastonbury Mountain rises to the west and, by walking to the left a bit, you can see Mount Snow to the east.

The picnic area is just down the road to the right.

Suspension Bridge across East Branch River

Somerset Reservoir

Somerset Reservoir

The Pinnacle

5. The Pinnacle

Class: II
Elevation: 425 feet
Vertical rise: 280 feet
Distance (round trip); .8 miles
Hiking time: ½ hour

A check of old maps indicates that the Pinnacle was formerly called Plum Hill—after the Plum family who lived nearby. Its modern name, however, is a bit misleading: it is little more than a big hill. Its head rises alongside the winding Connecticut River in Weathersfield.

The Connecticut River used to be a prime source of drinking water for domestic animals. Although cows come to mind first when we think of Vermont farm animals today, sheep were the state's principal livestock in the 1830s. William Jarvis, the American consul in Lisbon, imported the first Merino (i.e., longhaired) sheep to the United States in 1811 and bred them for forty-eight years on his farm in nearby Weathersfield Bow. This brought about significant changes in the woolen industry, and stimulated the growth of sheep raising in the East.

Families will find this a pleasant outing. A wide, gradual path leads lazily upward. With its elevation of 425 feet, the climb doesn't promise you wide, far-reaching views. But the open overlook nestled between the summit's

Chipmunk

snowy, white birches directs your gaze to the peaceful Connecticut River Valley and rolling New Hampshire hills beyond.

The Pinnacle is a part of Wilgus State Park. From the junction of Vt. 44 and U.S. 5 in Windsor, drive south on route 5 for 6.1 miles to the park entrance on the left. Pay your 25¢ day-recreation fee (tent and trailer sites are available too) and park in the designated area to the right. Cross route 5 and walk to the trail's start just north of the park entrance.

This blue-blazed trail begins gradually, and quickly makes a switchback upward to the left. Paralleling the road below, you follow a wide, flat trail between stands of hardwoods. In the fall you may identify these trees by the leaves and fruit they shed on the ground. The oval, blunt-based leaves of the birches turn yellow in autumn. The coarse-toothed, egg-shaped leaves of the beech are light brown and often veined with yellow. Long, lobed leaves—usually light brown—and familiar acorns, announce the presence of oaks. White pines spill their five-clustered needles onto the trail.

After this long, gradual stretch

The Pinnacle

of walking, you start a swing to the right. The hillside drops off steeply to the left. Hemlocks appear frequently along the trail. The shorter, irregularly-arranged needles help distinguish them from the balsam fir. Tiny cones and rough bark further identify these evergreens.

Stands of slender, white birches predominate as the path bears right. These tall, striking trees are accented by the soft green of intermingling white pine.

At approximately .2 miles the blue blazes mark a sharp right turn onto a narrower trail. Watch carefully here: the wider trail you have been following continues straight ahead.

Birds abound. Watch for the hermit thrush—the Vermont State Bird. This songbird can adapt to a variety of habitats. It may live in swamps or dry uplands, overgrown pastures or thick woodlands. Though the hermit thrush exhibits a marked preference for coniferous forests, it will also abide in predominately deciduous ones. This brown bird's white breast is speckled with flecks of brown. Its bell-like song is especially pretty. The call is a low clucking, followed by a mewing sound. When disturbed, it shows

its displeasure by slowly raising its tail.

The path swings right to make one long, final ascent. This is the steepest section of the hike. Winding upward, the trail passes a simply-constructed, stone slab bench.

Make your way over natural stone steps as you continue to climb. The trail traverses the slope from right to left, then turns right and heads straight for the summit.

After cresting two small slopes, the path turns right. From here it is a short walk to the small clearing which is the top of the Pinnacle. A blue blaze completely encircling a white birch marks the summit.

A semi-circle of birch trees and ferns edge this open area. There is ample room to stretch out and enjoy the pastoral setting which unfolds to the east.

The Pinnacle

6. Mount Hor

Class: II
Elevation: 2,648 feet
Vertical rise: 748 feet
Distance (to both overlooks and back): 3.1 miles
Hiking time: 2 hours

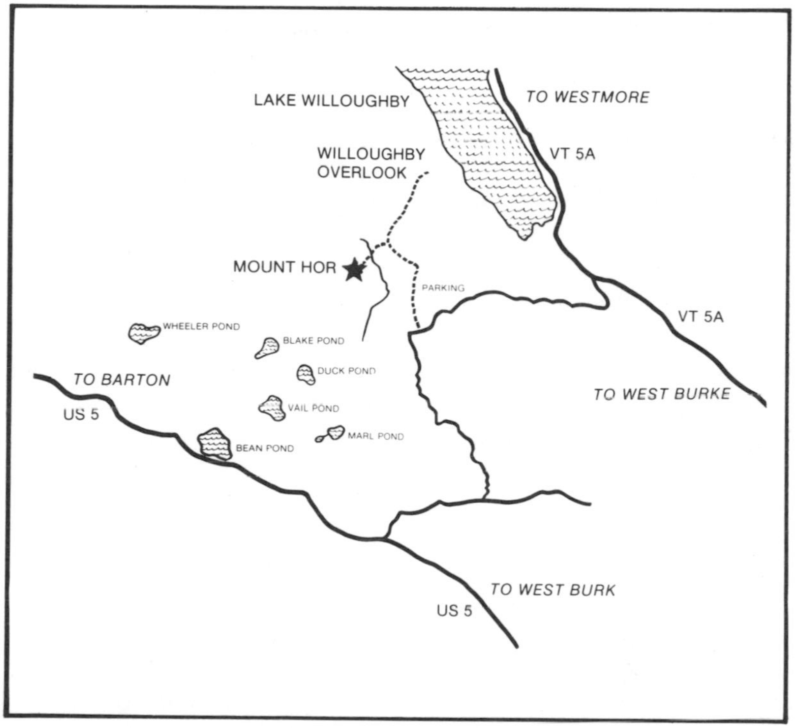

The Mount Hor Trail, located in Willoughby State Forest (see Hike 39), is a good one for leisurely leg stretching and relaxed enjoyment of panoramic views.

The hike is gradual, making it an ideal trip for families and beginning hikers. The views will appeal to everyone.

Much of the land in this forest has been logged out quite recently, causing an absence of mature trees. Following the common practice, the State of Vermont purchased the land for a reasonable price. This wise method of procuring large tracts has made a beatifully primitive area available for public use.

Hor is one of three mountains with summit trails in the Willoughby State Forest. Accordingly, its trails are maintained by the Trail Committee of the Westmore Association. This group provides a valuable and much needed service—asking, in return, only that hikers cooperate by not spreading litter along the trails. In fact, why not carry a small bag with you and collect whatever rubbish you come upon.

The access road to Mount Hor

Multi-zoned Polystictus

lies on Vt. 5A, 5.7 miles from both the junction of Vt. 5A and U.S. 5 in West Burke and the intersection of route 5A and Vt. 16 in Westmore. Watch for the brown and white "Willoughby State Trail System" sign on the west side of the road. Pull in here and follow the gravel road through the woods for 1.8 miles.

A white sign on the right identifies the Mount Hor parking area. After leaving your car, walk

south along the road approximately 150 feet to the start of the trail on the right.

The way begins as a narrow, rocky path leading gradually upward through dense side growth. Blackberry bushes edge the trail. If you happen by in the late summer, their tangy sweetness is yours for the picking.

The trail rises briefly and then flattens out. Its sides are dense-

Mount Hor

ly covered with young maples, elms, and birches, and with goldenrod. It is difficult to see beyond the edges of the trail because of the closely packed trees.

Winding slowly upward to the right, the path levels out again. Leg-brushing hillside growth reminds you that you are still on a very narrow route.

The path is marked by dark blue blazes, with occasional black-arrowed white signs lending assistance. The going gets rockier as you near the top.

Do you cancel a hike because of inclement weather? If so, we ask you to reconsider—especially since Mount Hor is a very walkable rainy day hike. Hiking in the rain produces a world of new experiences if you are properly attired. While it is necessary to pick your way more gingerly, the compensations are worth the effort. Rain beating on your body makes you feel more a part of the outdoor experience. There is also a grey-green softness to the woods during rain which is absent in sunnier times.

The trail begins an upward swing to the left over bare logs laid lattice-like across the path. They provide firm footing over the soft,

black mud beneath. Although the way climbs relentlessly uphill now, it is rock-free and quite easy going.

A massive, lightning-scarred beech tree stands to the right. The trail climbs straight and more steeply upward. Notice the sassafras growing to the right side. It is most easily identified by its forward-pointing three-lobed leaf. Clusters of dark blue berries ripen in September. Sassafras tea was a product of colonial times and oil of sassafras was once used widely as a medicine. It is still used to perfume soap.

At the .7-mile mark the trail reaches a junction. White signs guide you left to the summit (West Lookout) and right to Willoughby Lookout. Follow the left trail ¼ mile to the summit.

This winding, primitive spur is marked by pale blue blazes. You have to step around or over many trees and stumps. Shortly the path passes over a small streamlet. Continue on this rough route as it winds upward and dips into a clearing.

The view to the west encompasses ten small ponds in the valley below. They sparkle among

the heavily wooded areas of Willoughby State Forest. In the distant background, portions of the Green Mountains are also visible.

Return to the junction and go left. Follow the dark blue blazes .6 miles to the Willoughby Overlook. This trail is mostly flat and gradual. The way turns sharply right past a lone white birch and a small hemlock, and rises slightly. It levels out and passes a small gulch on the left. The path is soft and spongy as you pass downed trees festooned with turkey tail fungus (See Hike 8).

The trail climbs a slight incline; two white- and black-arrowed signs appear on the left. Swing right and down a short embankment.

A breath-taking vista—Mount Pisgah towering above the southern end of Lake Willoughby —unfolds before you. In the distance, parts of the White Mountains can be seen.

Return to the trail junction and follow your original route back to your car.

Mount Hor

7. Prospect Rock

Class: II
Elevation: 1,050 feet
Vertical rise: 530 feet
Distance (round trip): 1.5 miles
Hiking time: 1 hour

View from Prospect Rock to Mount Mansfield

This hike curls pleasantly through cool woods, then climbs upward for the last invigorating ¼ mile to the rock. It's a satisfying trip for everyone. Experienced hikers should not omit this one because of its brevity or small vertical rise. Prospect Rock's 1,050-foot vantage point offers a prime view of the Lamoille River Valley, with the Sterling Range in the background. You can also survey the northern slope of Mount Mansfield to the south.

Prospect Rock is on the Long Trail. To reach the access to this section of the trail drive west on Vt. 15 from the junction of Vt. 100C and 15 in Johnson. After 1.8 miles bear right onto the Johnson-Waterville Road. This turn is just before the Lamoille River Bridge. Drive .9 miles on this road to the Ithiel Falls Camp Meeting Ground on the left. Directly across the road the Long Trail leads north up the hill and into the woods.

There is very limited parking

Prospect Rock

along the side of the road in front of the campground. More parking is available at the off-the-road area .2 miles east.

The Ithiel Falls Camp Meeting Ground has been in existence for over seventy-five years. Each summer the Nazarene Church sponsors a non-denominational gathering of people from across the country at this lovely location. Camping here is available only to church members.

Follow the white blazes of the Long Trail up the incline and into the woods. A brown and white sign indicates that you are on the Long Trail North heading for Prospect Rock. Shortly after mounting the crest of this incline you cross a quick-flowing brook. Don't be surprised to see it pass across the path two more times.

This first part of the trail is a rather broad, gradual path through the woods. Abundant greenery edges the way: for example, the hay-scented fern. Common at lower elevations, it also grows in the alpine forests. It thrives in moist, partially shaded areas. The dry fronds exude the fragrant odor of hay.

Logs offer footing through occa-

sional soft, black, muddy areas. You make your way up the narrow, gently inclined trail. Numbers of knee-high red spruce crowd the path.

The trail dips into the subdued light of an older stand of spruce. Footsteps are muffled by spruce spills over the soft earth. Sun glows softly through the thick web of branches and past the limbless reddish-brown trunks.

Ahead the trail begins a sudden, steep climb through open woods. A rugged hiking stick will serve you well here. When you reach the top of this slope, bear to your right. Mushrooms and shining club moss border the trail.

Very soon you'll walk out onto Prospect Rock. Although there is no sign to mark this ledged area, you will readily recognize it by the views which stretch before you.

Return via the same route.

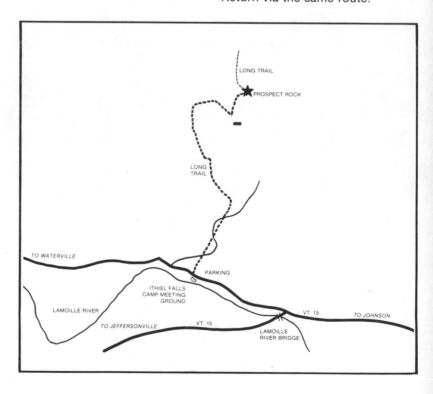

Prospect Rock

Southern Vermont

The summit of the Dome

The Dome

A tangy treat awaits you about three-quarters of the way up this trail: wild raspberries stand ready to delight your tastebuds, and add a special bonus to this hike.

This gradual-to-moderate climb scrambles over ledge as it nears the Dome's summit. Once there, you'll see how this mountain got its name: a massive bulk of rounded ledge swells upward out of the surrounding terrain.

From the junction of U.S. 7 and Vt. 346 in Pownal, drive south on route 7 for 2.6 miles and turn left onto Sand Springs Road. Follow it, bearing right as the road forks, for .6 miles. Go left onto White Oaks Road. Drive 1.4 miles, past the Broad Brook Trail, to an old road leading into the woods on the right. This is the start of the Dome Trail. Park off the road here.

Blazes for the Dome Trail are orange painted over white—resulting in a creamy color (a few of the white blazes, though, have not been painted over). The trail is well marked and easy to follow.

The old road becomes grassy and passes through an open field. It crosses between lines of aspen and leads through a second

8. The Dome

Class: III
Elevation: 2,748 feet
Vertical rise: 1,648 feet
Distance (round trip): 4.6 miles
Hiking time: 2½ hours

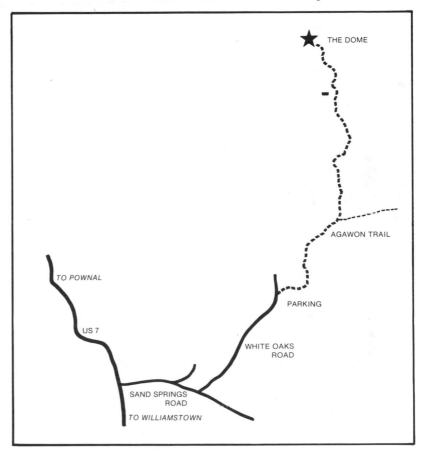

field. Re-entering the woods, it becomes both level and smooth. The way proceeds gradually upward. Large-toothed aspen and birches dominate the woods with their respective greenish-yellow and white trunks.

Climbing a moderate grade up to the left, the road becomes rutted and rocky. Walking is easiest along the left side here. The way turns sharply left after cresting this grade and passes along the ridge top.

After ½ mile you come to a three-way fork. Follow the Dome Trail to the left. It makes a quick swing back to the right and continues over rocks and roots. At times the trail gouges into the earth as it struggles upward.

Another fork appears at .7 miles. Look closely and you'll see that the two paths rejoin up ahead. Follow either one.

Large rocks fill the trail as it winds up through young woods. Countless thin trees swarm around occasional older, thick ones.

The Agawon Trail branches off to the right at 1.0 miles. Continue straight here. Note the numerous oak trees throughout this area. The acorns from these

trees provide food for songbirds, grouse, mourning dove, deer, bear, fox, raccoon, squirrels, and chipmunks.

Scattered pines edge the trail as it climbs gradually below a ridge line. They are red pines, identifiable by their three-to-

eight-inch needles in clusters of twos. The bark plates have a reddish tinge and the needles lift upward on branch ends.

At 1.4 miles the trail intersects with another old road. The remains of a junked truck mark this spot and indicate that,

The Dome

in the not-too-distant past, these slopes were the site of much more activity than is indicated by their present virgin appearance. Turn right and follow the road through a section of woods clogged by numerous downed trees.

Another trail branches left at 1.5 miles as you ascend a moderate slope. Rocks fill the way once again. Cresting a short, steep slope you see masses of ledge above to the right.

The path loops around behind the ledge and begins a short, steep climb. Dead beech trees support hundreds of multi-zoned polystictus. These pore fungi have thin leathery fans marked by dull-colored, concentric bands. Because of their beautiful markings, they have been nicknamed "turkey tails."

The light grey smoothness of beeches fills the woods on both sides of the trail. Various-sized rocks in the path make walking a bit adventurous. The gradual-to-moderate incline continues.

An old grassy trail branches right at 1.8 miles. Go straight ahead here. Cross several small brooks and climb up along the edge of a slope as the hill-side rises steeply above.

The path jogs sharply left and passes many raspberry bushes. The arching, reddish branches have prickly thorns. White flowers appear from May through July and the red fruit ripens from June through October.

You'll be returning by the same route. If you plan much berry-picking it can wait until then.

As you climb higher, the trail twists and turns through evergreens. Spruce and balsam thicken the woods from ground level to towering heights.

The path winds around and over pieces of ledge. You step up onto a small cone of ledge surrounded by evergreens—and may think this is the top. It's not. Climb down the other side and follow the blazes up onto open ledge, amidst more spruce and balsam.

The summit lies atop a large section of smooth, humpy, white ledge lined with orange-brown streaks. Trees surround this area and block views to the north and east. To the west are the Adirondacks and south is Mount Greylock in Williamstown, Mass.

The Dome

9. Harmon Hill

Class: II
Elevation: 2,123 feet
Vertical rise: 963 feet
Distance (to summit and back): 4.2 miles
Hiking time: 2 hours

It is best to do some limbering up before this particular climb. Otherwise, the steep beginning of this short hike will leave you surprised and breathless. Just before the half-way point the grade slackens noticeably and remains gradual the rest of the way.

The open, grassy summit of Harmon Hill allows good views to the north and west from its southwestern-corner-of-the-state vantage point. It also invites you to spread a cloth for a picnic lunch or to stretch out on your back for cloud watching.

From the junction of Vt. 9 and Vt. 100 in Bennington, drive east 3.8 miles on route 9. Turn south at the east end of the highway bridge crossing Walloomsac Brook, and drive down into a small clearing. Park anywhere here, but don't obstruct the dirt road which continues beyond the clearing.

Walk from the parking area along the dirt road. White blazes show the way. After a short distance the trail turns left off the road and leads straight up a steep embankment. Cresting this slope, the path continues

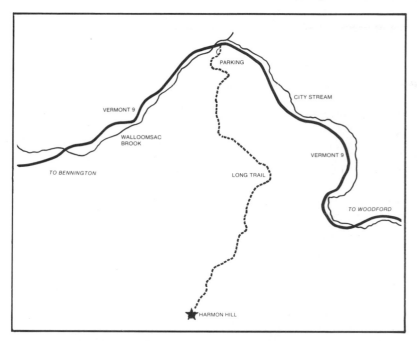

quite steeply up the hillside.

At .2 miles the trail joins an old road and swings sharply right. It follows this rocky road upward, becoming more gradual as it gains elevation. After 200 feet the trail leaves the road and continues up the slope to the right. Next, it swings sharply left onto still another road, then proceeds up a moderate incline bearing back to the right.

At .3 miles the way makes a switchback to the left onto another road. At the top of a rise

it bears around to the right. Soon the trail narrows down to a packed dirt path.

After .6 miles you cross an open swath beneath power lines. To the right you can glimpse the city of Bennington. This is a lower elevation preview of the prime views from the top of Harmon Hill.

Swinging left onto yet another old road, the trail makes a slow, rounded swing to the right. It bears left and climbs moderately along the eastern slope of an

Harmon Hill

unnamed hill. Here thorny shrubs tug at your clothes.

A long stretch of muscle-straining walking marks your approach to the ridgetop above to the right. After cresting it at 1.0 miles, you travel through a relatively flat area of open woods. Deciduous trees and evergreens are scattered over this hilltop.

Spruces and balsams hug the trail closely as it curls through this flat area. The path leads between hardwoods and thick shrubs before emerging into the open.

Ravens have been spotted in this area. They are larger than the common crow, with a wing span reaching to four feet. They frequently glide in flight, wings fully extended. At home along the seacoasts as well as inland, these omnivorous birds have adopted a favorite seagull trick. They will break open shellfish by dropping them onto rocks from high above.

Meandering through fields of tall grass, you walk out onto rounded ledge at 2.1 miles. A signpost officially marks this spot as Harmon Hill, elevation 2,123 feet.

Mount Anthony (2,340 feet) rises above Bennington which spreads below to the west. The city's historic battle monument towers pointedly from its center. Glastenbury Mountain is the 3,748-foot giant to the northeast. Almost due north, and closer, is Bald Mountain. Trees rim the other exposures of the summit and obstruct views in those directions.

View from Harmon Hill to Bennington; Mt. Anthony beyond.

Harmon Hill

10. Mount Olga

Class: II
Elevation: 2,415 feet
Vertical rise: 515 feet
Distance (around loop): 1.7 miles
Hiking time: 1 hour

The hiking trail to Mount Olga begins in Molly Stark State Park (in Wilmington)—named for the wife of General John Stark. Molly gave vital and historic aid to her husband during the Battle of Bennington in 1777.

In the first week of August of that year she received an urgent missive from the General:

"Dear Molly: In less than a week, the British forces will be ours. Send every man from the farm that will come and let the haying go."

In addition to the men from their own farm, Molly rounded up two hundred others to join General Stark in battle. For her reward, she received a brass cannon, one of the six British cannons captured by the triumphant Americans during the battle.* (The Molly Stark Cannon is now displayed in the New Boston, New Hampshire, town library. It is pulled along each year in that town's Fourth of July parade. After the parade the cannon is fired to commence the afternoon activities in the park.)

While not as historically fam-

*From a brochure on
Molly Stark State Park; Vermont
Department of Forest and Parks.

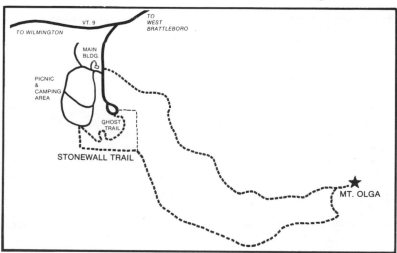

ous as "Molly," Mount Olga also became known as a result of a generous individual effort. Olga Haslund deeded the mountain to the State of Vermont with the understanding that it would be named after her.

To reach Molly Stark State Park drive east from Wilmington on Vt. 9 (The Molly Stark Trail). The park entrance is 3.4 miles from the junction of Vt. 9 and Vt. 100 in Wilmington. Drive to the administration building to pay your 25¢-per-person-per-day facilities fee. Ask about the best place to park.

Follow the grassed-in road which starts to the left front of the administrative build-

ing and travels south to a small clearing. The white-blazed Ghost Trail leads to the right here. Follow it.

This packed dirt trail curves around to the right and passes near a log park building. It descends through a shallow gulley past the remains of an old stone wall. Swinging sharply right, the path bends around a lone glacial boulder.

The trail makes looping switchbacks to the left and back to the right. After .2 miles it emerges onto one of the park roads. To the left, a brown and white Mount Olga Fire Tower sign directs you back into the woods.

Mount Olga

Along the trail to Mount Olga

Follow the blue- and white-blazed trail which parallels the continuing stone walls. It swings 90 degrees to the left and follows a fairly straight path. The gentle dips and rises of this (appropriately named) Stone Wall Trail mean pleasant walking.

After .3 miles of hiking you pass over a walkalong. There will be a few more boggy areas to cross before the trail reaches a junction at .4 miles. Here the Stone Wall Trail turns left. Go right onto the blue-blazed trail leading to Mount Olga's summit.

A representative inhabitant of this area is the distinctively plumed barred owl. Its head, neck, and upper breast feathers form dark bars across a lighter-colored background Since this owl's small feet are not large enough to capture sizeable prey, its diet consists mainly

Mount Olga

of mice—which it catches in open country near its home deep in the woods.

Try answering the barred owl's call (four evenly pitched hoots, then the same repeated), or make a squeaking sound with your mouth against the back of your hand. One of these large, inquisitive birds may appear in a nearby tree at any time of day to carefully inspect you with its dark brown eyes.

The wider, blue-blazed trail leads upward more steeply. Occasional rocks or small boulders must be scrambled around. To the sides of the path are open deciduous forests dominated by beech trees.

After slabbing the slope to the left, the way levels out and passes between two giant sections of ledge. Becoming narrower, the path passes red blazes on the right at .8 miles. These mark the boundary line of Molly Stark State Park.

The path frequently twists and turns through short evergreens as it approaches the top of Mount Olga. Just below the summit a blue-blazed trail joins from the left. This will be the return route of your loop trail to the

fire tower. Go right to an old road and turn right again. Follow this road to the summit.

Transmitting antennae, three small buildings, and a fire tower crowd the small, open summit. From the tower you can scan the surrounding countryside in all directions. Three peaks are particularly prominent. Hogback Mountain (2,410 feet) is in the near northeast. To the northwest is 3,462-foot Haystack Mountain, and 3,556-foot Mount Snow is to the north-northwest.

Follow the path back down the old road and left to the junction of the two blue-blazed trails. Go right here. Your descent, though moderately steep at times, is cushioned by the evergreen spills which thickly cover the path. The trail sides teem with spruce and balsam fir.

At 1.3 miles the way leads through a stone wall. This is still a quietly pretty trail. The sound of your steps is muffled by the needles covering the path. The light filters softly through thick branches.

At 1.4 miles this trail intersects with another which joins from the left. Go right here and continue down the slope.

In contrast to the deciduous woods you passed through on the way up, the return route has meandered down through an endless evergreen forest. Small, bushy "youngsters" are scattered amongst the taller, slimmer parent trees. There are also a few thick-trunked "grandparent" spruces.

At 1.6 miles the way cuts through another stone wall. Soon you cross a wooden-planked bridge across a small brook. The trail then steps up to the park road just across from the administrative building.

Mount Olga

Haystack Mountain

11. Haystack Mountain

Class: III
Elevation: 3,462 feet
Vertical rise: 1,242 feet
Distance (round trip): 2.4 miles
Hiking time: 1½ hours

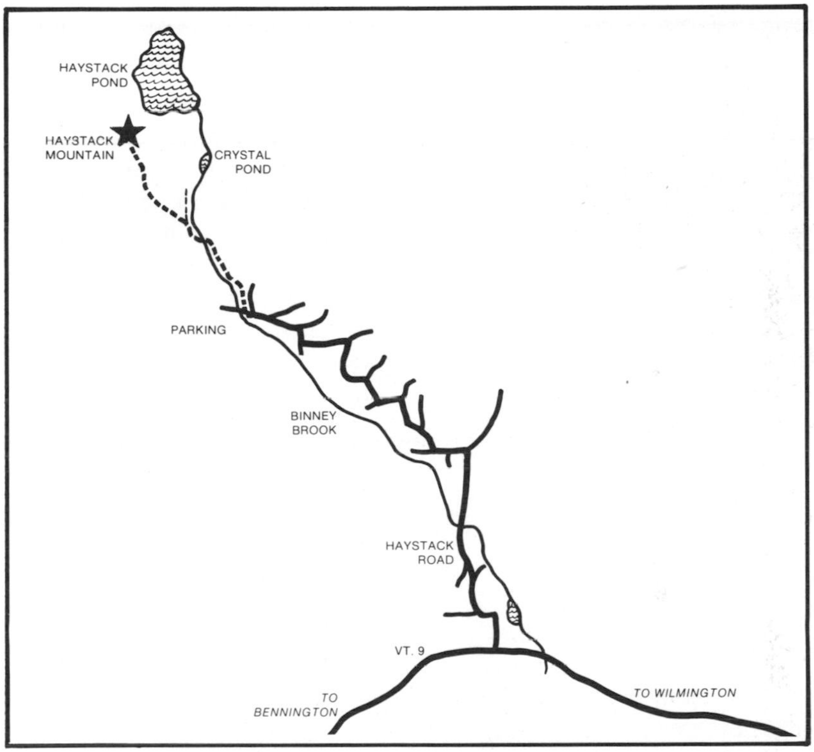

Prepare for a picnic, and a sun-soaking, on the summit of Haystack Mountain. A brief but rugged ascent takes you to its small, evergreen-enclosed peak.

You begin using your "path finding" skills early as you search for the start of the Haystack Mountain Trail. Some years back there was a fairly direct route to the trail, north of Vt. 9. However, the spread of civilization in general and the rise of a community of new houses and roads in particular make finding the trail's start a bit more challenging today.

From the junction of Vt. 100 and Vt. 9 in Wilmington, drive west on route 9. After 1.1 miles, turn north onto Haystack Road at the Chimney Hill sign. Follow this road for 1.2 miles to another Chimney Hill sign. Turn left here onto Chimney Hill Road.

Take the next right onto Binney Brook Road. Follow its turning, angling path past Howe's Loop, Large Maple Way, Lila Lane, and the upper end of Howe's Loop. At the "T" intersection with Twin Chimney Road go right

Red Squirrel

and continue to the next "T" intersection. Go left onto Upper Dam Road.

Drive past Rocky Split Way and another (unnamed) road. Just beyond on the right the Haystack Mountain Trail begins. Park along the edge of this wider section of road.

A small, brown, yellow-arrowed sign and some fluorescent orange arrows direct you up this

dirt road as it leads away from Upper Dam Road at a 30-degree angle.

A remarkably friendly group of chickadees may herald your arrival. Whistle their chick-a-dee notes and they may venture closer for a noisy inspection. Both black-capped and the smaller, brown-capped variety may be seen, although the brown-capped species favor higher elevations.

Haystack Mountain

Both species prefer to nest in natural cavities or old woodpecker holes in rotten stumps. They feed primarily on insects.

The old dirt road climbs moderately from Upper Dam Road. Although somewhat rutted and rocky, it is smooth enough to let you set a rhythmic pace. At about .1 miles another old road joins from the right. Continue straight and make your way around or under the car chain across the road.

There are no blazes to direct you along the occasionally boggy road. However, the way is well-cleared and the narrower trail which ascends to the summit is a well-beaten one.

The vertical rise along the road is consistently gradual. At .4 miles the trail swings slightly right. Below the embankment to the left you can see the waters of Binney Brook.

A culvert guides the brook's journey beneath the trail. Beyond this point the slope of the road increases. At .6 miles the road forks right. Bear left onto the narrower trail leading up the mountainside.

This unblazed trail curls up over rocks and small boulders.

Winding to the right, the path maintains a steadily demanding pitch. Beyond a sharp bend to the left, it becomes even steeper.

Trees protrude from a jutting section of ledge ahead as the trail swings right below it. Continuing up this southern slope of the mountain you pass through a section where the trail has gouged and gutted its way upward.

You're likely to see animal droppings atop the small boulders in and around the trail. Weasels are one animal noted for depositing their scats on these rocks. Also, they tend to use the same spot again so there may be both old and new accumulations. There will be pieces of fur and bone in their slender two-inch droppings.

Nearing the summit, you pass through an area fragrant with evergreens and glistening with birches. Shortly before the top the trail levels out and bears sharply right.

The needle-covered path emerges onto the summit at 1.2 miles. The small, ledged area nestles within a circle of evergreens. A flat, grassy section invites you to stretch out in the sun.

Climb up onto the highest piece of ledge to examine the views. Over and between the trees you can see 3,605-foot Mount Snow to the north. Wide, bare swaths of ski trails scar its slopes. The lofty blue shape on the northeast horizon is Mount Ascutney. Directly below to the northeast is Haystack Pond. This is the water supply for the town of Wilmington.

Far to the east you can see New Hampshire's 3,165-foot Monadnock Mountain. To the south is Harriman Reservoir. In the distant southeast is 3,491-foot Mount Greylock, the highest point in Massachusetts. Much of the view to the west and north is blocked by trees.

When ready to return, remember to bear left at the fork as you step down off the summit. Then follow the same route by which you ascended.

View of Scott Covered Bridge & Bald Mountain

Haystack Mountain

12. Bald Mountain (Townshend State Forest)

Class: III
Elevation: 1,680 feet
Vertical rise: 1,140 feet
Distance (around loop): 2.5 miles
Hiking time: 2 hours

"Bald" is by far the most popular name for Vermont's tree-less peaks. Whatever the reason for such popularity, Vermont's "Bald Mountains" must be further identified by their geographical locations. This hike takes you to the summit of 1,680-foot Bald Mountain in the Townshend State Forest.

The short, steep climb to this peak will challenge those in above-average physical condition. If you are not in good shape, this climb could be downright humiliating and possibly unwise to attempt. The trail rises 1,140 feet in only .8 miles.

On Vt. 30 drive 2.5 miles south

from the steepled white church in West Townshend or 2 miles north from the junction of Vt. 30 and Vt. 35 in Townshend. Go west onto the narrow steel bridge at the Townshend Dam.

This impressive structure was built between 1959 and 1961 by the U.S. Army Corps of Engi-

Bald Mountain

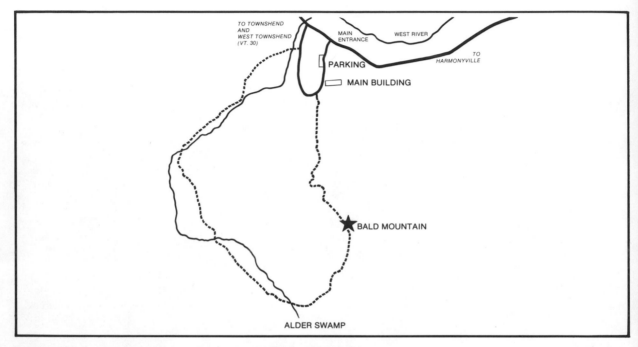

TO TOWNSHEND
AND
WEST TOWNSHEND
(VT. 30)

MAIN
ENTRANCE

WEST RIVER

TO
HARMONYVILLE

PARKING

MAIN BUILDING

★ BALD MOUNTAIN

ALDER SWAMP

neers, to control flood waters in the Connecticut River Basin. It is operated for the protection of downstream areas in Vermont, New Hampshire, Massachusetts, and Connecticut. During the record storms of June 30–July 4, 1973, it held back millions of gallons of water, thereby preventing possible loss of life and heavy damage in downstream communities.

Follow the road over the bridge and dam to its end and go left. Just before turning sharply right

the road approaches the Scott Covered Bridge. Built in 1870, this is the longest single span (165.7 feet) of its type in Vermont.

Turn right at the main entrance of the Townshend State Forest Camping Area (1.7 miles from the dam). Park in the big lot that appears on your right as you approach the main building.

The short, steep climb begins just behind the main building. It passes a large, solitary stone fireplace on the left and heads upward. Rocks and roots slow the

pace as you begin to feel the angle of the slope.

At .2 miles the trail crosses an overgrown path. Note that the forested areas here are very young. Most of the trees are slender, light grey beeches.

The trail turns sharply right onto an old grassed-in road at .3 miles. Almost immediately it turns left and resumes its upward climb.

Approaching thick stands of ever-

Bald Mountain

greens, the path becomes even steeper. The incline rather than the footing is what makes progress so laborious.

Tall hemlocks (with occasional white birches peeking through them) fill this unusual area. The dark roughness of tree trunks and cold greyness of ledge are softened by gentle green hemlock needles.

Small spruces line the trail as it levels out at .6 miles. Legs and lungs receive a short rest before the way swings left and up once again. The next ¼ mile to the top is a little less steep but climbs over more ledge and large boulders.

Throughout this climb you will see small ground-level caves dotting the hillside. Formed by rocks piled together, they provide ideal homes for porcupines.

The flat summit is composed of ledge and grass. To the right is an open vista looking northwest. Stratton Mountain dominates the left side of this view. Return to the trail and follow the sign to the south vista. Actually looking southeast, you peer down into a valley through which the West River passes. Across a high ridge line are tiny distant peaks. New Hampshire mountains poke their heads up on the left horizon.

Follow the blue blazes down the gradual south side of the peak. The path steepens somewhat and then flattens out. White pine needles cushion the way.

Approximately ¼ mile from the summit the trail passes an alder swamp on the left. These trees are closely related to the birches and have white cross marks on their brown bark. In the eastern United States they are shrub or small tree size. The leaves have short stems and strong, slanted veins. Beavers use alders for both food and building materials.

The trail narrows and passes down through a lane of tall, scraggy pines. Then, at 1.4 miles, it passes around and under the overhanging limbs of an ancient white birch. So thick is the trunk of this old-timer that any of its six main branches would be "tree size" by themselves.

Descending easily, the trail reaches the red-blazed line of boundary markers for the state forest. The path makes a sweeping turn to the right and passes through the opening in an old, moss-greened stone wall.

Just beyond are a number of tamaracks. Also known as larches, these conifers lose their leaves in the fall. Their inch-long needles grow in tufts at the end of dwarfed branchlets and have a furry look. The tamarack's seeds, inner bark, and needles provide food for a variety of woodland creatures.

Passing through more evergreens, the trail begins a long, fairly steep descent to the brook below. It swings right and parallels the water before crossing it at 2.1 miles.

Don't be surprised if you see trees with exceptionally large leaves through this area. The basswood linden has eight-inch leaves that are sharply-toothed and unequally heart-shaped at the base. This is a tree with many by-products. Its soft wood is used for excelsior and lumber. American Indians made rope from the tough inner bark and medicinal tea from the fruit. The flowers are a good source of honey.

The trail continues its descent beside the brook. At 2.5 miles it crosses back to the other side and joins with a dirt road. Go right at the fork here and return to your car.

Bald Mountain

Mount Equinox

13. Mount Equinox

Class: IV
Elevation: 3,816 feet
Vertical rise: 2,861 feet
Distance (to summit, Lookout Rock, and back): 6 miles
Hiking time: 4 hours

Many legends have been handed down about this mountain's name. A popular but fictitious one centered around Captain Partridge, one-time director of the American Literary and Scientific Academy. During the autumnal equinox on September 19, 1823, the captain marched a group of cadets to the summit, where they conducted barometric measurements. Most probably, *Equinox* derives from the Indian word "Ewanok" meaning "the-place-where-the-top-is."

Mount Equinox is the highest mountain in the state not on or adjacent to the Long Trail. At 3,816 feet it is also the highest peak overlooking the Vermont valley, extending from Bennington to Rutland.

Because of malaria in the lowlands and the Indians' fear of high mountains, nineteenth-century settlers populated the slopes of Equinox. During those times the mountain teemed with trails. Lack of interest and need however, have allowed them to become overgrown. Today only the Burr and Burton Trail ascends directly from the valley to the

View from summit of Mt. Equinox

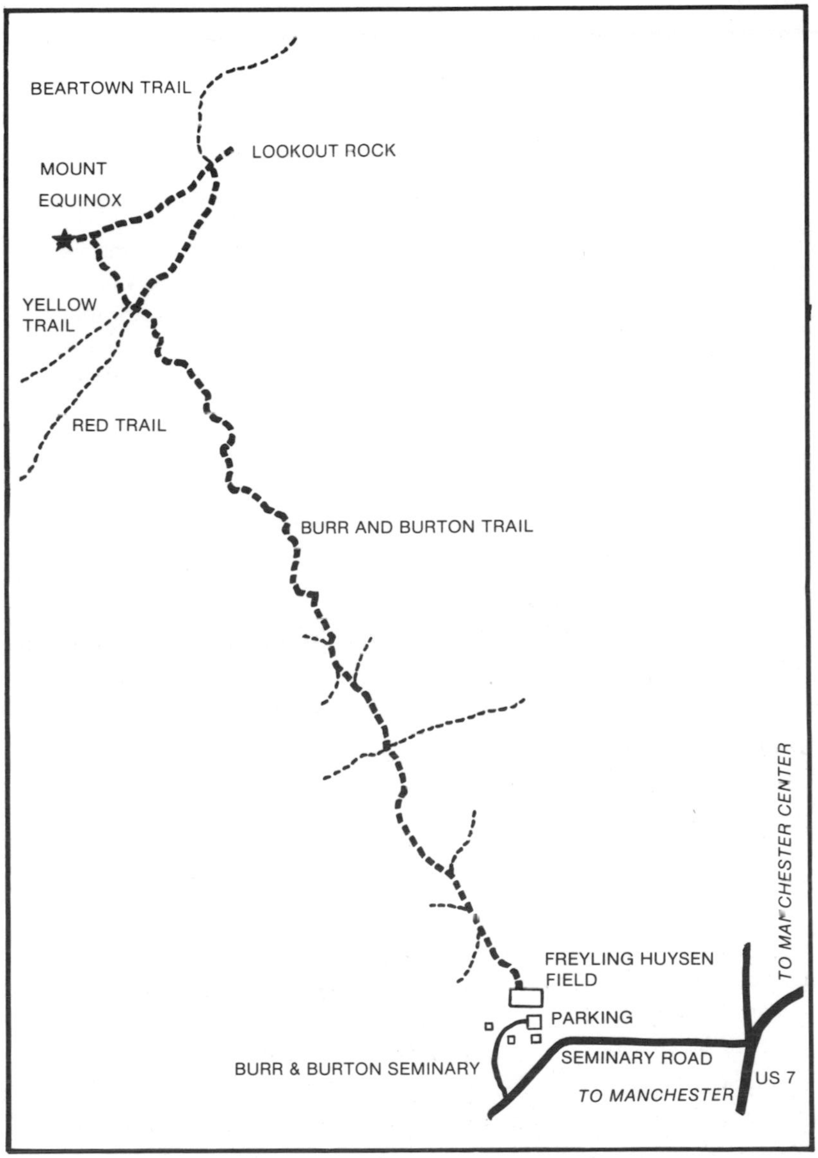

BEARTOWN TRAIL

LOOKOUT ROCK

MOUNT
EQUINOX

YELLOW
TRAIL

RED TRAIL

BURR AND BURTON TRAIL

TO MANCHESTER CENTER

FREYLING HUYSEN
FIELD

PARKING

SEMINARY ROAD

BURR & BURTON SEMINARY

US 7

TO MANCHESTER

Mount Equinox

summit. (Two others connect the Sky Line Drive Toll Road with Lookout Rock.)

The climb up the Burr and Burton Trail begins gradually, but soon becomes challenging. You'll want to be physically ready for this one before starting out. Legs seldom get a rest. Many trees cross the trail, forcing you to climb over or crawl under them. The path is well marked near the bottom, but the blue blazes disappear as you go higher.

From Manchester, drive north on U.S. 7. Take the first left onto Seminary Road. Follow it to the front of Burr and Burton Seminary. Continue on Seminary Road as it bears around to the left here. Take the next right into the driveway which leads up behind the school into a large parking area.

Climb up to the athletic field above the parking area. Cross to the far side toward the left corner and watch for the well-beaten path. Unsigned, but blue-blazed, the Burr and Burton Trail begins here.

The flat, needle-covered trail winds gradually upward beneath white pines. It joins with an old road and continues straight. As the incline steepens, a yellow-blazed path exits left.

The rutted road forks at .4 miles and the trail goes left. Climbing the moderate slope, you switch back to the right and cross over an intersecting road at .6 miles.

Thick stands of striped maple line the way. At .7 miles follow the trail left at a fork. Another path joins from the left rear before you bear right at the next fork.

You can now forget about watching for forks in the trail and turn your attention to the running ground pine along the path's edges. This creeping evergreen is actually a club moss. It is used for Christmas decorations and is commonly referred to as princess pine.

As the trail switches back to the left and loops widely right, its pitch increases. From here to the summit, you are in for a relentless uphill trek.

Passing through many white birches, the path makes a long traverse up to the left. It narrows suddenly and squeezes past a glacial boulder at 1.3 miles. Quickly returning to its wider ways, it again climbs steadily.

Evergreens cloak the hillsides as the path begins a wide swing to the right. Footing becomes less sure as it narrows. The slope steepens even more.

The sides of the trail rise as it turns right. This rock-filled, shallow gully is a haven for lush greens. Mosses, lichens, and ferns fill the evergreen-shaded path.

After a series of short turns the trail makes a long, steep climb to the left. At 2.1 miles it ends the sharp uphill pitch and bends slowly right. It becomes surprisingly gradual before gaining elevation again.

Make your way up through body-brushing balsams past the "NO TRESPASSING" signs (these apply not to hikers but to hunters, trappers, and people carrying firearms). Just beyond, several trails intersect (at 2.5 miles). Pass by the red trail on the left and follow the yellow arrow ahead. After a few feet bear right onto the trail to the summit.

The next ¼ mile to the summit passes through continuing stands of evergreens. Cross an old road at 2.6 miles and climb to the junction with the Lookout Rock Trail. Go left across open ledge to the summit. Ahead is the

Mount Equinox

Equinox Sky Line Inn.

By circling the inn you can see for miles in all directions. On the far horizons you can look into New York State, Massachusetts, and New Hampshire. On a clear day, Mount Royal in Montreal is also said to be faintly visible.

Looking north and east you can see Dorset Peak, Killington Peak, Bromley Mountain, Magic Mountain, and Mount Ascutney. To the south, Stratton Mountain, Mount Snow, and Glastenbury Mountain are prominent. The Adirondacks rise to the west.

Also located on the summit are Federal Aviation Agency peripheral communications stations.

These radio towers enable planes to contact Boston's Logan Airport for landing instructions. An educational television station built by the University of Vermont transmits near the Lookout Rock Trail.

When you are ready to descend, return to the Lookout Rock Trail and follow it .4 miles to Lookout Rock. This is a fairly easy walk over some rock and through evergreens. A small clearing along the way contains a memorial to Mr. Barbo, the dog of Dr. J.G. Davidson, former owner and developer of much land on Mount Equinox.

From Lookout Rock you can look down into the Vermont Valley. Stratton Mountain looms to the right and Equinox Pond sits directly below you.

Leaving this vantage point, bear left onto the yellow trail and follow it .4 miles to the junction with the Burr and Burton Trail. Turn sharply left onto this unsigned trail and return via your original route to your car.

Mount Equinox

Bromley Mountain

14. Bromley Mountain

Class: III
Elevation: 3,260 feet
Vertical rise: 1,320 feet
Distance (round trip): 4.6 miles
Hiking time: 2½ hours

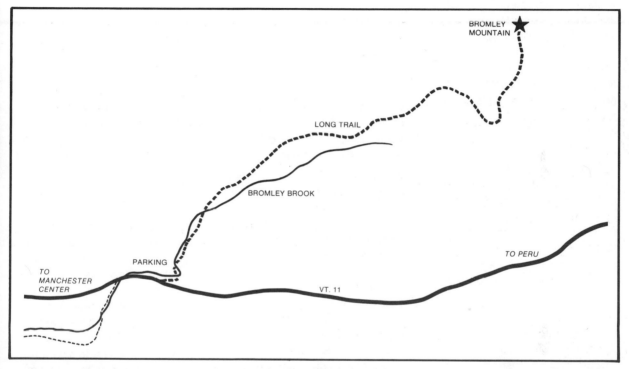

This is a two-in-one hike. The greater part is a gentle woodland walk. The last third is a steeper, slower climb. You can meander or stride for about a mile and a half before settling into the more arduous, muscle-tugging final climb of .7 miles.

The trail to Bromley Mountain begins at the Long Trail crossing of the Manchester-Peru High-

Bromley Brook

way (Vt. 11). Drive east 5.9 miles from Manchester Center, or west 4.4 miles from Peru. Turn north at the trail sign and park at the widened edge of the dirt road.

Walk approximately 150 yards down the road. At the sign for the Long Trail, turn left into the woods. Follow the well-beaten path across the steel footbridge over Bromley Brook.

The white-blazed trail leads very

gradually upward. Cut logs carry you across a wet area as the way flattens out. Step over the thin, weaving roots and small rocks that fill the path.

Sounds of moving water can be heard to the left. As you continue along, the rock-floored brook comes into view. Flashes of white water highlight its swirling, downward journey.

To the sides of the trail are the ever-present dead or dying trees

Bromley Mountain

which form an integral part of the forest's life cycle. They serve as hosts for various types of fungi—non-flowering plants which lack the chlorophyll necessary for photosynthesis and thus depend upon other organisms for food.

You can see examples of the rusty-hoof fome attached, primarily, to beech and birch trees. This three- to twelve-inch wide, cone-shaped fungus is a perennial that may grow for as long as thirty-five years. With each new year it adds a zone of tubes, called pore fungi, located on the plant's sheltered underside.

Walking gradually upward to the right, you reach another crossing of Bromley Brook at .6 miles. A raised, cross-logged footbridge provides rustic support here.

Rising up from the brook the trail becomes very flat as it winds through open woodlands. Occasional glacial boulders loom mutely among the trees. Their great bulks harbor the many greens of ferns, mosses, and trees.

The way leads past a wide, gentle, rock-free section of Bromley Brook on the right. A three-logged bridge carries you over a small streamlet on its way to the brook. Several other trickles of water must be stepped over, as you pass through this area.

At 1.3 miles a small hump of ledge interrupts the flatness of the path. The bright whiteness of this quartz-filled rock contrasts sharply with the dull brown of the packed-dirt path.

Watch for pleurotus mushrooms growing on living trees (they never grown on the ground). The oyster pleurotus grows in tight clusters and has 3- to 5-inch flared caps, one above the other. Gills form rib-like undersides. This mushroom is usually white or grey when young and becomes yellowish with age. We do not recommend sampling any of the mushrooms described in the hikes. Many edible and poisonous species look so much alike it is nearly impossible to tell them apart.

The trail approaches the brook again at 1.6 miles and swings away to the left. Your first taste of the remaining steep climb lies just ahead. After cresting a short ridge and temporarily leveling out, the path begins a serious ascent.

The way narrows as it begins a long, upward climb. Thick birches, maples, and beeches staunchly guard the edges of the twisting trail.

Huge boulders lean out from the hillside above as you climb diagonally to the right. Cresting the ridge, the path swings left across it and readies itself for the heights ahead. Rising steeply again, the trail passes through (predominantly) beech forests. It tops this ridge and flattens out once again.

The hairy woodpecker is common here. This black and white bird has a white breast and vertical stripes down its back. (The male displays a small red patch on the back of his head.) Its barb-tipped tongue can be extended into holes to reach the larvae of boring beetles. Not to be confused with the smaller, but similarly-marked downy woodpecker (six to seven inches long), the hairy woodpecker (eight to nine inches long), has a much longer, heavier bill, and it dwells primarily in forests.

Just before reaching a ski slope at 2.2 miles, the path crosses an unusual jumble of smooth-topped rocks. Look right (south) when you walk out onto the ski slope for a beautifully framed view of Stratton Mountain (ele-

Bromley Mountain

vation, 3,936 feet).

Turn left and follow the steep ski trail to the top of Bromley Mountain. A sturdy wooden observation tower offers fine views in all directions.

Close to the north is Styles Peak. Looking east you see many low rolling hills, with no outstanding peaks. Stratton Mountain is prominent in the south, and the high peak in the distance to the south-

west is Glastenbury Mountain. The Taconic Range looms impressively to the west. Hotel-topped Mount Equinox dominates the near west.

Your return will be by the same route.

View from Bromley to Stratton

Bromley Mountain

Baker Peak & Griffith Lake

15. Baker Peak and Griffith Lake

Class: III
Elevation: 2,850 feet
Vertical rise: 2,130 feet
Distance (round trip): 7.4 miles
Hiking time: 4 hours

This hike takes you through an area which was quite exclusive in earlier times. Vermont's first millionaire, Silas Griffith, built a lake house retreat on the body of water which bears his name to this day. He made his fortune from lumbering the forests around the town of Danby, although the town itself did not take on an air of prosperity until quarrying and dairying became established.

Expansive views from the summit of Baker Peak and a peaceful visit to the now-wilderness (Griffith) lake highlight this outing. The mileage makes this trek a real leg-stretcher, but there are no sections of tedious climbing. Even the open ledged approach to Baker Peak can be easily handled.

Drive two miles south from Danby on U.S. 7. Turn east onto a gravel road next to a small cemetery. Follow this road for ½ mile to the Green Mountain National Forest sign (for the Lake Trail) on the left. There is ample parking in an open field beside the sign.

Your walk begins on the Lake

View from Baker Peak west to Dorset Peak

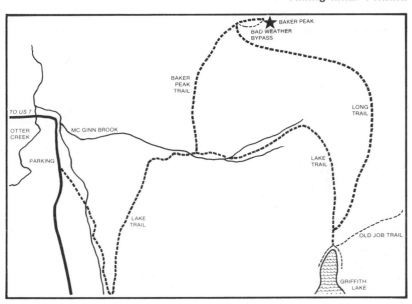

Trail and branches to the Baker Peak Trail. After leaving the summit of Baker Peak, you'll utilize the Long Trail South to Griffith Lake. The Lake Trail will return you to the parking area.

The blue-blazed Lake Trail leads right from the clearing and follows an old road. This was formerly the carriage road which led from the valley to the Griffith Lake House.

Pine needles cloak the trail as it leads gradually upward. Below the hillside to the left loud rushing of McGinn Brook can be heard.

After the initial gradual incline the trail levels out. At .2 miles it dips down to cross a fast-flowing brook. Now following its left bank, you continue gently upward beneath delicate hemlocks.

At .6 miles the path makes a rounded switchback to the left. This is the start of a long traverse which slabs moderately upward. The hillsides rise high above and drop off steeply below.

Long sections of smooth ledge form occasional walls above the trail. At 1.2 miles a sturdy bridge carries you across a gap beneath one of these steep ledge

Baker Peak & Griffith Lake

faces. The supports of an old trestle can be seen imbedded in the rock below.

Beyond the bridge the trail cuts along the side of a slope beneath continuing masses of ledge. Steadily climbing, it narrows and passes along a hillside flooded with white birches.

The way swings right and continues to curl around the hillside's edge. McGinn Brook's gushings become audible far below. Frothy white waters settle into quiet pools as the brook rises to parallel the trail.

At 1.5 miles you reach Ben's Bathtub. One of the larger pools along this trail, this lovely spot invites you to refresh yourself before traveling on.

Trails join just after you cross McGinn Brook at 1.6 miles. The Lake Trail leads right and the Baker Peak Trail heads left. Go left onto the latter (blue-blazed) trail.

The Baker Peak Trail makes a long, moderate climb along the mountain's western slope. The narrow path passes between brilliant slopes of white birches and leads just below the ridge line.

Swinging sharply right, the way

passes over rougher sections of loose rock and protruding roots. The trail becomes more gradual as it curves through thick stands of dwarfed birches.

At 2.4 miles you reach an open section of ledge. Looking left you can see U.S. 7 in the valley below. Dorset Peak, with its white quarries, rises commandingly beyond the highway.

The quarries were originally worked in the early 1800s. At that time the demand was for smaller cut stone to be used for hearths, doorsteps, and tombstones. With the advent of better transportation and equipment, larger stones were quarried.

The Baker Peak and Long Trails join at 2.5 miles. Their blue and white blazes follow the same route the final 500 feet to the summit. Just beyond this junction is the Bad Weather Bypass. This sheltered route is recommended when inclement weather makes the climb over open rocks hazardous.

The final ascent is a steady climb over a wide, smooth spine of rippled ledge. To your left is a tantalizing preview of the wide western view you'll witness at the top.

The summit is a tiny flattened area identified by a painted blue square. A sign just beyond marks Baker Peak's elevation at 2,850 feet.

A full semi-circle of views stretches out before you. In clear weather, sharp-peaked Killington and the rounded cone of Pico can be seen to the north. The Adirondacks are partially visible to the northwest. Dorset Peak is directly across, with Woodlawn Mountain behind to the right. Emerald Lake sparkles to the south. Netop Mountain and Green Peak back it up, while Equinox Mountain raises its lofty head just beyond.

Looking down into the valley, you see the town of Danby to the northwest. Route 7 slices along in a north-south direction at floor level. The looping bends of Otter Creek meander along the east side of this road.

Return to the junction of the Baker Peak and Long trails. Go left onto the Long Trail South. This route is consistently easy going. Level stretches alternate with gradual dips and rises.

At 3.3 miles you begin the first noticeable ascent as the path brushes by a large glacial boul-

Baker Peak & Griffith Lake

der. Farther on (3.6 miles) you cross a damp, boggy area via the raised roots of nearby trees.

The Long Trail intersects with the Lake Trail at 4.3 miles and swings left. Follow it approximately 500 feet through evergreens and birches to the northern end of Griffith Lake.

Sunlight dances on the water's surface as you approach. After passing the Old Job Trail on the left you reach the lake's shore. This quiet, primitive setting is an ideal spot to eat lunch and spend some time just lazing around.

When ready, retrace your steps on the Long Trail to its junction with the Lake Trail. Go straight on the blue-blazed Lake Trail. In 1½ miles this route will intersect with the Baker Peak Trail, and continue down the mountain to the parking lot.

The path flattens out as it passes through a grassy field. Then it crosses two tiny brooks and makes a sharp swing to the left.

At 5.2 miles the trail bears left onto an old rutted road, which it follows for approximately ½ mile down a long, gradual grade, crossing several tiny brooks in the process.

The road narrows to trail width as rushing brooks accompany it on both sides. They meet and swing left as the path crosses over them and shortly thereafter reaches the intersection with the Baker Peak Trail.

Go straight, across McGinn Brook, and follow your original route on the Lake Trail back to your car.

Along the Lake Trail

Baker Peak & Griffith Lake

Mount Antone

16. Mount Antone

Class: II
Elevation: 2,660 feet
Vertical rise: 850 feet
Distance (round trip): 4.6 miles
Hiking time: 2½ hours

Mount Antone lies within the boundaries of the Merck Forest (see Hike 2). This unique woodland and forest area contains twenty-six miles of hiking and cross-country ski trails for public use. Nine overnight shelters and many picnic sites are scattered throughout the forest.

There is no charge for using the forest but contributions are appreciated. Any money received is applied to future recreational and educational goals.

Everyone is requested to obey these rules:

1. All visitors must register.
2. No motor vehicles are allowed beyond the parking area.
3. Camping by permit only.
4. Fires allowed only in designated areas.
5. All trash must be carried out.
6. Hunting and fishing are permitted, but kills must be reported.
7. Only snowshoers and cross-country skiers may use the forest in the winter.

The entrance to the Merck Forest is located on Vt. 315 at the height-of-land between Rupert and East Rupert. Drive east

Wood Asters

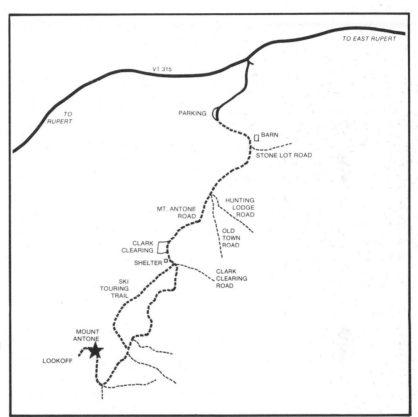

3.3 miles from the junction of Vt. 153 and 315 in Rupert, or west 2.6 miles from the junction of Vt. 30 and 315 in East Rupert. Turn south toward the brown and yellow "Merck Forest Foundation, Inc." sign.

Bear right at the fork and follow this road approximately ½ mile to the parking area. Walk the short distance to the information board, and register. Maps of the forest are available here.

Step over the chain next to the information board and begin to hike down Old Town Road. White birches surround the road as it leads gradually upward. After about ¼ mile, you come to a road junction (a large barn sits on the left). Turn right onto Mount Antone Road.

The trail dips between large areas of cleared land on both sides. Down to the right is Page Pond. You're likely to hear the quacking of wild ducks echoing from this tiny body of water.

Just beyond the pond you can look up to the right and see the humped dome of Mount Antone. The way rises slightly as young trees fill the hillside to the left. Open land to the right allows for an excellent view to the northwest.

Young forests cloak both sides of the trail as it rises gradually and then flattens out. Continued easy walking brings you to a sweeping left turn at .8 miles. Follow the curve to the open area.

Several trails radiate outward from this clearing. Before turning sharply right to follow the footpath leading to Mount Antone's summit, walk to the far edge of this cleared area. From here you can see Mount Equinox, with its hotel and transmitting towers.

Follow the grassy trail next to the Mount Antone Road sign. On the left you'll see a stand of

red pines with their characteristically uplifted branches. This northern tree has three- to eight-inch needles in clusters of two. It is often called Norway Pine, although it is native to North America.

Gentle dips and rises make for easy walking as the trail passes through hardwood forests. Many thin, young grey-barked beeches cover this area.

At 1.1 miles the way passes through Clark Clearing. Another clearing just beyond offers distant views to the west and the Adirondacks of New York State.

A quaint four-sided shelter comes into view on the right. Built of logs and set atop a stone foundation, it has tall, narrow windows (they were fashioned by leaving out vertical logs in appropriate places). Stumps and flat stones make the inside comfortable, while a front overhang keeps rain from the open door.

In front of the shelter is a four-way trail junction. The Mount Antone Road leads diagonally upward to the right (but just to the left of the ski-touring trail).

The steeper part of the hike begins here. The way leads up to the left across a slope and turns

right. A series of turns brings you to the crest of the ridge. The trail remains smooth and easily walkable through here, but the incline does offer some challenge.

The trail flattens out and crosses the ridge to the right. Just ahead, at 1.8 miles, the ski-touring trail rejoins from the right. Continue straight on the Mount Antone Road as the Wade Lot Road branches left.

Lookout Road is passed, after another 500 feet. The way bends around a small knoll on the right and begins a long, straight gradual ascent.

At 2.1 miles the path makes a sweeping switchback to the right. Leading left from the turn are the Beebe Pond Trail and Masters Mountain Road. The way rises more steeply as it climbs to the summit.

You enter the small, flat area at the top of Mount Antone after a hike of 2.3 miles from the information center. To the right (northeast) is a view overlooking much of the Merck Forest. The barn you passed earlier can be seen in the large clearing straight ahead. The three towering summits beyond are (from right to left): Dorset Peak, Woodlawn Mountain, and Tinmouth Mountain.

A narrow path leads off the far side of the clearing. Follow this a short distance to another cleared overlook. Look down into the valley and out across low, rolling hills. The cleared land and cows of scattered farms comprise this pastoral scene.

On a clear day it is possible to see westward as far as the Adirondack peaks of Mount Marcy and Whiteface Mountain.

On the return trip, take the ski-touring trail which branches off to the left after ½ mile. It descends moderately and straight along the side of the slope and will bring you back to the shelter. Remember to bear left here and then return to the information center by the same route you came up.

Caterpillar

Mount Antone

Natural Bridge

17. Natural Bridge

Class: III
Elevation: 1,700 feet
Vertical rise: 840 feet
Distance (round trip): 2.8 miles
Hiking time: 1½ hours

Imagine a deep gorge carved into solid rock by the relentless rushing of cascading water. Ragged edges show where rocks broke at their weakest points. The sides of the crevice flare freely upward in a V-shape. But somehow a slender span of rock has failed to crumble. It connects the sides of the gorge like a narrow catwalk. This is the natural bridge.

Don't be misled by the shortness of this hike. It is a rugged climb. The trail itself is easily walkable, but the steep incline keeps you leaning into the hill most of the way. Be ready for a good workout.

The many breathers that your heart, lungs, and legs will insist upon should provide excellent opportunities to observe the abundant plant and animal life of this area.

Turn west off U.S. 7 in North Dorset, into the entrance for Emerald Lake State Park. Don't go into the park. Instead, quickly bear right at the sign for the Natural Bridge. You'll find a parking area a short way down this road. The parking fee is

Natural Bridge

$1.00 for cars and $2.00 for trucks. Although this is a state trail, the land available for parking is privately owned. Should you prefer to leave your car in the State Park Area, you will pay only the park fee (25¢ per person) for using the day facilities. You will, though, have a longer walk to the start of the trail.

Just beyond the private parking area, a gradual slope bordered by open fields offers a pleasant beginning to this hike. In the ravine below to the left a rushing brook provides musical accompaniment as you wind your way upward.

After approximately ¼ mile the wide trail forks. Keep right here and ascend the very steep path ahead. Loose rocks make the climb up this pulse-quickening hill even harder.

Hemlocks arch their delicate branches across the path, as another trail enters from the right rear. These beautiful trees have more flexible twigs and branches than spruces or balsams, as well as tiny, perfectly-formed cones. Their bark is rich in tannin; woodsmen and Indians made tea from the twigs and leaves.

Reflectorized orange diamonds

Natural Bridge

identify this as a multi-purpose trail (open to hikers, cross country skiers, snowshoers, and snowmobilers). A barbed wire fence parallels the path, and seems to divide the forest. White birches abound to the right while evergreens occupy the left. The long, moderate uphill grade continues.

Swinging right, the wide packed-dirt trail becomes steeper. The sides of the path rise higher; your steps become more laborious.

You crest a long grade and swing sharply left. The grade lessens a bit as the trail makes a long, diagonal switchback to the left.

Rocks fill the trail as it continues relentlessly upward. Looking left through the trees, you can see a ridge line towering high above, across a deep valley. The mountains responsible for this high landmark are Dorset Hill, Netop Mountain, and Dorset Peak.

The trail swings sharply left as the hillside suddenly flattens out. The grade lessens. Legs get a short-term reprieve.

Red squirrels may chatter at you throughout this area. These vivacious creatures have a very small home range—usually within a small group of trees. They live in hollow trees; or, if these are not available, they build outside nests of grass and fine twigs and line them with shredded bark. In addition to gathering nuts and cones for winter storage, they place mushrooms high on tree branches to dry in the sun before tucking them away.

A dry brook bed is crossed at .8 miles. The trail cuts across the slope here and remains fairly flat. Deer tracks can be seen in the soft dirt. Whitetail deer most often leave separated, two-toed tracks, although sometimes they appear as single, heart-shaped prints. You may be fortunate enough to see one of these beautiful creatures or at least its raised white flag (tail) as it runs from you. A sharp snort or whistle will also signal the presence of deer.

Just before beginning to rise again, the trail passes over a jumble of large white limestone rocks.

Ferns begin to appear along the sides of the trail. Two unusual kinds grow abundantly here. The maidenhair fern has finely divided, horseshoe-shaped leaves. The Christmas fern is slender from base to tip with a scaly leafstalk, stiff leaves, and spiny leaflets.

A wide trail joins from the left rear at 1.1 miles. Note this junction well. On the return trip you will bear left onto the narrower trail and return to your car by your original route.

The presence of a stone wall on the right side of the trail will alert you to an approaching turn. At the end of the wall, follow the blue blazes steeply downhill to the right. The narrow path leads directly to the natural bridge.

The two-foot-wide stone bridge is roughly two feet thick at the sides and tapers to one-foot thick in the middle. Walk out onto it, for a refreshing change in perspective. It connects the rocky hillsides above the floor of the gorge. Water flows through here only during the spring run-off now.

Natural Bridge

18. Little Rock Pond and Green Mountain

Class: IV
Elevation: 2,509 feet
Vertical rise: 1,849 feet
Distance (round trip): 5.6 miles
Hiking time: 4½ hours

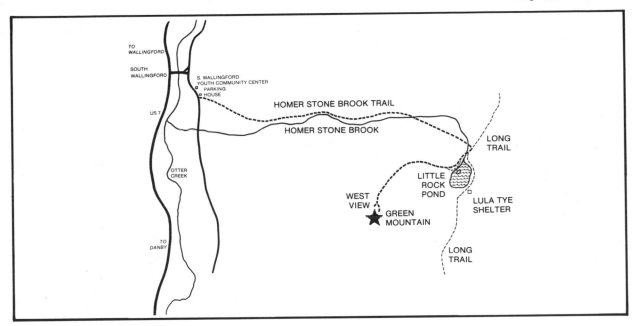

Give yourself plenty of time to enjoy this wilderness pond and mountain. The area teems with wildlife and you won't want to rush. A quiet wait can reward you with lots of animal sightings. And besides, it's nice to bask in the sun atop the ledges of Green Mountain.

If an overnight stay fits your plans, you can sleep at the Lula Tye Shelter, located on the Long Trail at the southeastern tip of Little Rock Pond. A spring nearby provides fresh water for the six to eight hikers this shelter can accommodate.

You'll reach your destination via the Homer Stone Brook Trail. To get there turn east off U.S. 7 just south of the South Wallingford Union Congregational Church. Drive .2 miles across a bridge and around a righthand curve to a red building on the left. This is the South Wallingford Youth Community Center. Park beside it.

The Homer Stone Brook Trail begins behind the next house on the left (N.B.: No parking allowed near this house). Walk up the driveway and around to the right of the house.

The trail begins by following the old South Wallingford-Wallingford Pond Road. The way leads up a moderate grade. Stone walls and open fields flank the road. Blue blazes and occasional arrows mark the way.

After ¼ mile the road makes a wide swing to the right. Keep on this packed dirt road and bypass the path leading left at the bend.

Maintaining its gradual slope,

Little Rock Pond & Green Mountain

the road leads up between bordering hemlocks. These evergreens dust the trail with their tiny needles and miniature cones.

Beyond the hemlocks, the way passes through an open deciduous forest. A massive, gnarled maple guards the left side of the road as another trail leads left. Stay on the road.

Walking is enjoyable up this gradual incline. You make a brief aromatic passage through a small area of hemlock and white pine.

After .6 miles you can hear the rushing waters of Homer Stone Brook below to the right. Follow the road as it bends right and passes by still another trail leading left.

Now the way parallels the brook. Clear water pours through boulders trying to choke its flow. Rippled pools form amongst the rocks.

Above to the left the hillside slopes steeply around eroded cliffs. Quaking and large-tooth aspen and beech cling tenaciously to the slope.

For a short stretch the brook drops down into a shallow ravine. You can hear it foaming and surging along below the road.

Farther along the road and brook

parallel each other at the same level. At approximately 1.3 miles the way crosses the Homer Stone Brook, leaving the South Wallingford-Wallingford Pond Road. Rounded stones carry you over the flowing water.

Bear sharply right after crossing the brook. Walk about 100 feet, turn sharply left and begin to climb up the gouged-out slope.

Very quickly you top a small mound of earth as the trail joins with an old road. Turn left here. Mark this junction well so that you will not pass by it on the return trip.

This grassy road cuts upward and across the slope to the left. Small rocks clutter the path and make progress slow at times. Homer Stone Brook rejoins the trail near the top of this long incline.

The trail crosses over the brook and reaches the junction with the Long Trail at 1.9 miles. Go right and follow the white blazes toward Little Rock Pond.

A blue-blazed trail appears quickly on the right. Turn here and follow it over rough-hewn logs bridging the brook's northern outlet. Follow the blue blazes along the pond's western shore.

Isolated Little Rock Pond is a

resting place for mallards, Canadian geese, and other waterfowl during their spring and fall migrations. Approach its shores with care and you may see one of these species before their wary senses make them fly off.

Mallards are bottom feeders. They submerge their upper bodies in shallow water in quest of plant growth. You will see them "tip up," with their tailends pointing skyward. Recognize the drake by his iridescent green head, white neck ring, white-edged, blue wing patch and curled tail feathers. The hen shares the blue wing patch but is dappled in shades of brown.

The large Canada goose is black-necked with a white marking (running like a strap from ear to ear) beneath its head. These birds feed on pond plants and on the grass or grain of open fields. In flight, they align themselves in various V formations. "Honking" usually signals the approach of their flying wedge long before you can see it.

The path gently dips and rises along the pond's western shore. Ahead you can see a small island. After you pass the point of the pond's northern outlet, with the island still visible ahead of

Little Rock Pond & Green Mountain

you, the blue-blazed trail to Green Mountain leads right.

The ascent to Green Mountain quickly becomes steep. A narrow dirt path climbs upward through hardwoods. Multi-zoned polystictus (a fungus with a shape and coloration resembling turkey tails) flare from the surface of dead tree limbs at the sides of the trail.

At the 2.3-mile point the path flattens out and descends briefly. It then swings sharply right. The trail continues its curvaceous ascent through thick stands of beeches. The forest floor is cloaked with verdant fern growth.

The way passes over a long rocky spine of ledge at 2.4 miles. To those who share our habits of imagination, this ledge resembles the back of some fairy tale monster.

You'll have to hoist yourselves up, using both arms and legs, over the continuing series of ledges. There are intermittent views to the east from open-ledged areas as the trail twists through thick, evergreen scrub growth.

At 2.7 miles the path forks. A spur leads right to the West View. Go left here and continue toward the summit.

One-tenth of a mile farther brings you to the open, rounded ledge at the summit. A blue circle marks the spot. Views include an easterly look to Little Rock Pond below, Homer Stone Mountain, and the smooth, waved crests of other mountains beyond.

Return by the same route.

Mallards

Little Rock Pond & Green Mountain

View of White Rocks Mountain and Cliff

White Rocks Cliff

19. White Rocks Cliff

Class: III
Elevation: 2,662 feet
Vertical rise: 1,622 feet
Distance (round trip): 3.2 miles
Hiking time: 2 hours

You are not at White Rocks Cliff when you reach the highest point of this hike. The spur trail to the cliff follows a rugged, ¼-mile downhill route. Once there, you'll enjoy a vantage point with panoramic views to the north and west. There is also a near view of a limestone rock slide below the mountain's north-west face. About the turn of the century, water coursed down the mountain, causing the whole side to slide off. There are actually three distinct slides, all of which can be seen from across the ravine.

Drive east on Vt. 140 from Wallingford. Bear right onto a side road after about 2 miles. Follow it 500 feet to the sign for the Green Mountain National Forest: White Rocks Picnic Area. Turn in here and proceed straight on this road to the picnic area and parking lot at the end.

The blue-blazed Keewaydin Trail leads out of the parking lot's far end. This wide trail begins with a gradual walk between picnic tables and two small Forest Service structures. Off to the left you'll hear the sound of a rushing brook. The trail swings right, up and away from the brook.

White pine have shed their five-

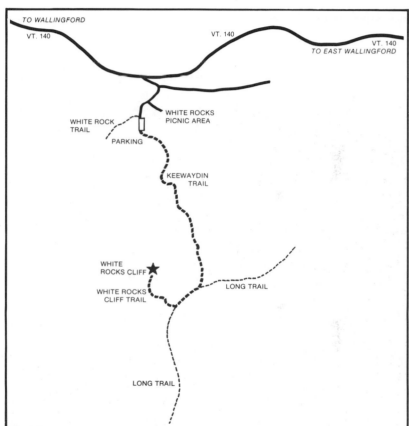

fingered needles across the path. After cresting a rise, you approach a stream and swing left before it.

A steady upward grade is maintained through white birch, large-tooth aspen, oak, and maple. Below and to the left you can hear the brook again. Look carefully for an opening in the trees. Through it you'll have a limited view of a small but very attractive cascade.

The trail swings right around a thick, shadowy stand of spruce, balsam, and hemlock.

After briefly paralleling the ridge line to the left, the path cuts up and across it. A short row of "bog logs" has been laid across a mirey section here.

Great glacial boulders loom in the open woods. Loose rocks fill the trail. Step slowly to avoid careless falls.

The return to a packed dirt trail makes the footing more certain. You legs and feet appreciate this, as there are few other respites from the unvarying upward grade.

At 1.1 miles the Keewaydin Trail joins with the Long Trail. Go right onto the Long Trail South. Frequent white blazes guide your way.

There are gentle dips and rises to the Long Trail as it follows the west side of a ridge. Stands of spruce and balsam engulf the way. Evergreen spills litter the path. You may want to pause along this sheltered trail to enjoy the surrounding quiet and isolation.

At 1.3 miles you reach a sign for the White Rocks Cliff Trail. Here a blue-blazed path leads right. Make your way carefully over the numerous loose rocks of this steep, rugged descent.

The trail changes to packed dirt and continues its steep drop through conifers whose needles color the slope brown. Twisting and turning through large boulders and ledge, the path makes a final descent to the cliff.

Here there are two flat areas for overlooks to the north and west. The town of Wallingford is most prominent to the right. Tinmouth Mountain rises straight ahead in the first ridge line. The second, higher ridge line is that of the Adirondacks of New York State.

Directly below you is one of the great white limestone spills. This type of rock is still processed in a nearby plant. It is used as a base for toothpaste and as an ingredient in lead-base paint.

(After returning to the parking area via the same route, you may want to explore the White Rock Trail. This blue-blazed trail leads southwest from the other end of the parking lot to an outcropping of ledge below White Rocks Cliff. From this vantage point you can see the cliff and all three white rivers of rock which cascaded down its side. The round-trip walk on this ½-mile-long switchbacking trail takes ½ hour.)

White Rocks Cliff

20. Mount Ascutney

Class: III
Elevation: 3,150 feet
Vertical rise: 2,370 feet
Distance (around loop): 0.0 miles
Hiking time: 4½ hours

Mount Ascutney has long been a focus of activity. Scalping parties foraged through this area in the eighteenth century. The first American mountain hiking trail ascended its slopes. Today, the mountain boasts a four-mile-long road to the summit (it is said to be one of New England's most scenic highways) and many ski trails. Small-plane and glider pilots use its distinctive shape as a convenient landmark.

During the French and Indian Wars bounties up to £100 were paid by both the English colonies and the French, for enemy scalps. Colonial scalping parties frequented the area around Mount Ascutney and used to climb to its summit to watch for smoke from Indian campfires.

In 1825 the people of Windsor opened the first trail up the mountain—making Ascutney the first American mountain to have an established hiking trail. Later trails and shelters provided sufficient inspiration for James P. Taylor to found the Green Mountain Club and to initiate the blazing of the 262-mile Long Trail. The Long Trail prompted others to create the 2,000-mile Appalachian Trail, which stretches from Maine to Georgia.

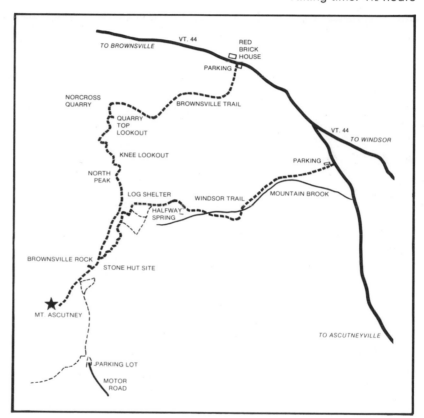

Three major trails lead to Mount Ascutney's summit. The Weathersfield Trail, which was recently revised to eliminate some of its rough sections, ascends from the south. The other two routes climb from the northeast; they will make up your loop tour of the mountain described here.

Remember that the starting points for these two trails are separated by .8 miles of black-topped road. You have the choice of parking where you plan to begin or (as we prefer) parking where you will finish, and walking back along the road to the starting point.

Drive 3.4 miles west on Vt. 44

Mount Ascutney

from its junction with U.S. 5 in Windsor, and turn diagonally back to the left onto an intersecting road. Follow this for .3 miles to a small house set back on the right. A sign on a fencepost identifies the Windsor Trail.

The owners of this property have offered portions of their land as parking areas for Mount Ascutney hikers. This is where the hike will *end*. You may leave your car at the edge of the lawn, under the trees, or in the scrub land further up the road between the white birches. It is expected that in return for this privilege you will take your trash with you when leaving.

Head back to the paved road and go left. From here it is .8 miles to the beginning of the Brownsville Trail. At the junction with route 44 go left. Follow this road to a red brick farmhouse on the right. Just before this house you will spot the Brownsville Trail sign on the left.

White blazes mark the trail as it follows the long, flat, well-beaten path up across the open field. Entering the woods the trail suddenly narrows and slithers through thick stands of hemlock. The branches overlap above, forming a natural tunnel.

You are now on the old Norcross Quarry Road. It rises gradually over packed dirt and loose stones. The hillsides become very steep to both left and right as the trail slabs the mountain.

Cross a jumble of rocks flowing down over the trail like a stone waterfall, and continue upward through more hemlocks. The incline lessens here but the footing is less certain as the way becomes filled with loose stones.

At approximately 1.7 miles from your car you pass a section of ledge rising steeply to the left. Water trickles over the rock all year long, forming a giant sheet of ice during the winter months. During the spring run-off it becomes a gorgeous waterfall.

Farther along you recognize Norcross Quarry by the masses of large rock along the trailsides. Climb up on the pile to the right for a view of valleys, rolling ridges, and distant peaks. The long, thick wooden remains of a derrick and rusted steel cables evoke the past.

The Norcross Quarry was the most extensive of the four quarries on Mount Ascutney. It produced the sixteen polished columns for the Columbia University Library and the thirty-four large columns for Canada's Bank of Montreal. During its several years of operation, however, it did not produce stone completely free of trace iron. Thus, the stone did not weather well; the quarry's backers went bankrupt.

The trail continues beneath overhanging ledge. It winds steeply upward between hunks of ledge and turns sharply left, then right. It becomes steeper as thick stands of evergreens gather along the edges.

A sign at 2.1 miles marks the Quarry Top Lookout. The short blue-blazed spur trail leads onto a flat ledged area above Norcross Quarry. From here you have a wide view to the north.

After passing through thick stands of evergreens back on the main trail, you'll see an arrow directing you to a revised route at 2.4 miles. It leads more steeply up the mountain over packed dirt, many rocks, and roots. From here to Knee Lookout you follow the path over a long series of diagonal traverses up the slope.

At 2.8 miles you arrive at Knee Lookout, with a view to the east. Continue to twist and turn another ¼ mile up the mountain until you reach a flat grassy area.

This is North Peak: elevation 2,660 feet.

Just beyond this peak you have occasional views to the west, through dead trees. Particularly prominent to the northwest are the pointed peak of Killington and the cone of Pico.

Trees shorten as you climb steadily upward toward Mount Ascutney's 3,150-foot summit. At 3.6 miles you reach the junction of the Windsor Trail. Keep right.

The Stone Hut remains occupy the clearing 500 feet further on.

You can still see the large slabs of granite used to construct the former shelter. Built in 1858 by volunteers, it was destroyed by vandals, rebuilt in the early 1900s, but later destroyed again—primarily by college students, who carved their initials in the metal roof with pistol bullets.

View to Mt. Ascutney across Windsor-Cornish Covered Bridge

Mount Ascutney

Leading to the right from this clearing is Brownsville Rock. From here you have a long view to the west and north. Open farmlands sectioned off by trees rise to mountain bases. Mount Mansfield and Camel's Hump are visible far to the north, while the Coolidge Range shows up clearly almost straight ahead. A bit south is Shrewsbury Peak. Salt Ash and Okemo Mountains are the closer peaks to the left.

Return to the clearing and go right .3 miles to the summit. A lookout tower and accompanying horde of antennae greet you as you crest the last ledged area. Climb the tower for a fine 360-degree view of the surrounding countryside.

From the summit it is 2.6 miles back to your car. Walk back down the Windsor Trail Junction and go right. The way twists and turns through stands of evergreens and scrubby birches, to the junction with the Blood Rock Trail after 4.7 miles (from the beginning of the hike). Keep left on the Windsor Trail.

Becoming rock-free, the path cuts across the slope and switches back to the right. It traverses the mountain and comes to another route junction. Go left toward the Log Shelter.

This rustic structure was built in 1968 by members of the Ascutney Trails Association. Two sides of the three-sided shelter are built of logs and the third is ledge and stone. It has three wire-bottomed bunks, a fireplace and a picnic table. Spring water in front completes the natural setting.

The Half Way Spring and the joining of the Blood Rock and Windsor trails are reached after 5.2 miles. The spring water is said to remain constant at a temperature of 39 degrees.

After a long series of traverses across the slope, the trail becomes more gradual. It passes between thick stands of slender maples and becomes filled with loose rocks. The pitch increases as you descend to Mountain Brook at the 5.5-mile mark.

Swinging left, the trail parallels the brook on the right. It descends over long hunks and slabs of stone as the brook drops lower into the ravine. Continuing beside the brook, the trail begins a long, straight, moderate descent.

The loose rocks disappear as the path widens and is ceilinged by hemlocks. Sides of the path open momentarily, and become filled with fluffy white pines. At 6.5 miles, a grassy road goes straight and the trail forks right. You are now just a short walk through blazing white birches from your car.

Mount Ascutney

Central Vermont

Milkweed

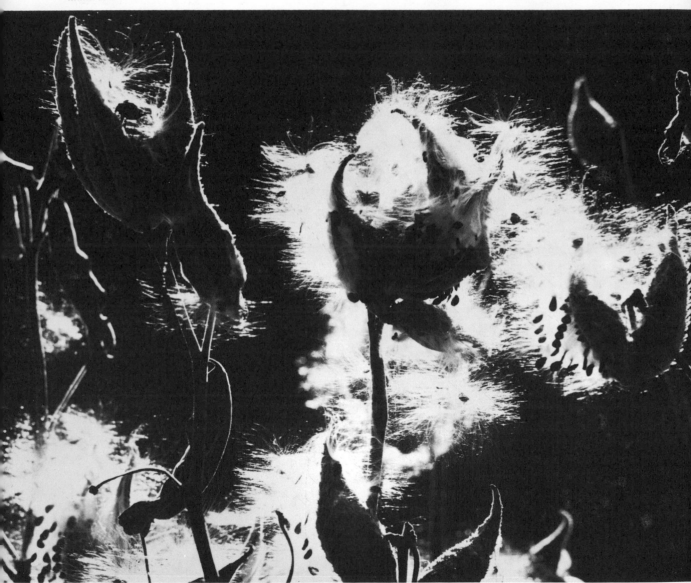

Slack Hill

21. Slack Hill

Class: II
Elevation: 2,200 feet
Vertical rise: 542 feet
Distance (around loop): 3.1 miles
Hiking time: 1¾ hours

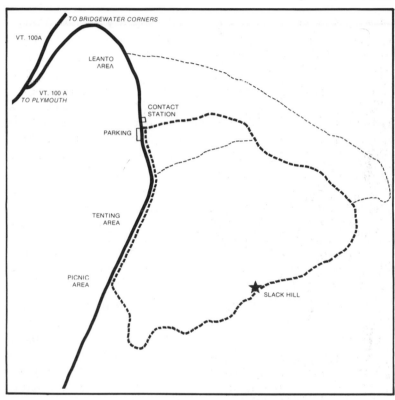

The leisurely woods walk to Slack Hill's summit takes you through the 3,400-acre Pinney Hollow area of the rambling Calvin Coolidge State Forest, which covers 12,000 acres, divided into several separate parcels.

Whether camping at the park or here for the hike only, you'll enjoy the wide trails, gradual slopes, and open wooded areas. Allow plenty of time for an unhurried, relaxing walk.

From Bridgewater Corners drive 4.2 miles on Vt. 100A to the entrance of the Calvin Coolidge State Forest. (Plymouth, the tiny community where Calvin Coolidge was born, lies two miles further south. The Coolidge Homestead is open to the public.)

Follow the long, winding road from the park entrance to the Contact Station (admission and information booth). Pay the 25¢-per-person charge for day use of the facilities and park in the area to the right. The blue-blazed trail begins behind and to the right of the booth. A longer trail (see map) begins back nearer the entrance of the park. However, it is used primarily as a pulp road (timber is harvested to insure proper management of trees and other vegetation) and does not have the scenic appeal of the footpath.

Your route is divided into three separate sections. The long, gradual climb to the top of Slack Hill is 1.35 miles. A descent of about a mile brings you to the parking lot at the picnic area. Another downhill walk (just under a mile), along the road connecting the picnic area with the Contact Station, will return you to your car.

The wide packed-dirt trail leads gradually upward through thin young trees. Occasional clumps of fern and slender striped maple are the only major ground cover between the tree trunks.

After topping the incline, the path levels and begins a series of short dips and rises. The trail becomes so wide open that it is possible to wander off the path. Keep an eye on the frequent blue blazes.

After ½ mile an arrow points back to the Contact Station and woodshed. Follow the blue blazes sharply left here.

This area supports a wide variety of animal life. You might be lucky enough to see any of the following: chipmunks, red squirrels, partridge, woodcock, deer, or rabbits. Songbirds also flourish; particularly the inquisitive chickadee. To attract the black-capped chickadees try kissing the back of your hand or whistling chick-a-dee-dee-dee.

The trail begins to slab gradually across the hillside. It continues to pass through typical hardwood forests, with only a scattering of the elms that were once prominent in them. The American elm seeds are eaten by grouse, squirrels, and opossum. Deer and cottontail rabbits browse the twigs. Unfortunately, this familiar tree is rapidly succumbing to Dutch elm disease.

After passing between thick stands of white birch, the path drops down through a wide open area and joins with a spur trail from

the left. A sign here points left to "Blueberry Leanto." Swing sharply right.

Unusual clumps of maidenhair fern appear to the right of the trail. The finely-divided leaves are four to sixteen inches wide and shaped like horseshoes. Individual leaves look like feathers in an Indian headdress as they waver in the slightest breeze.

The trail winds across the hillside and at the 1-mile point steps over an old stone wall. It becomes narrower and climbs toward the summit. Thick stands of red spruce and carpets of wavy broom moss flank the path.

Follow the flat, slowly winding trail to the summit. A brown sign marks the elevation at 2,200 feet. There are no views from here but you enjoy a peaceful relaxed feeling as you meander through these evergreens.

Follow the blue blazes past the elevation sign and descend gradu-

ally, .9 miles to the picnic area.

Single logs imbedded diagonally in the dirt occasionally cross the trail. This system of erosion prevention directs rain and snow run-off to the sides of the trail and keeps the flat path in fine condition.

Nearing the picnic area the trail makes a switchback to the right. It winds between thick areas of white birches and red spruces. Glimpses of parked autos through towering white pines signal the end of the woodland trail. Go right onto the road and follow it .85 miles to your car.

Slack Hill

22. Shrewsbury Peak

Class: III
Elevation: 3,737 feet
Vertical rise: 1,757 feet
Distance (round trip): 3.6 miles
Hiking time: 2½ hours

To Shrewsbury Peak

You leave the clutches of civilization before beginning this hike. No horns or screeching tires pierce the quiet as you start the roller coaster-like climb to Shrewsbury Peak. With each step the quiet of the forest grows deeper. Evergreen tunnels diminish thoughts of the world you left behind. Silent mountains await your company at the summit.

Take Vt. 100 from either West Bridgewater or Plymouth Union to the dirt road leading west, .2 miles south of the tip of Woodward Reservoir. This road can be recognized by its exceptionally wide entrance, beside the brown post and wire guard rails of Vt. 100. Follow it 3.3 miles to the short dirt road which, in turn, leads to the log shelter at the former Northam Picnic Area. (Just before reaching this turn there will be a narrow dirt road on the right. Go past it and take the next right.) The blue-blazed trail begins behind and to the left of the shelter.

Before you've gone very far, you'll notice the unusual trees beside the trail. Their dense conical shapes reach almost to

Shrewsbury Peak

the ground. One-sixteenth- to-one-eighth-inch long scale-like leaves hug the twigs and branchlets of the flattened sprays. The bark is very fibrous, with many cross ridges. This tree—the northern white cedar—is a stranger to most of the hiking trails in this book.

The northern white cedar grows in limestone soils and swamps, where it provides a favorite winter yarding area for deer. Moose, snowshoe hares, and cottontail rabbits also eat the twigs and foliage. Songbirds and red squirrels devour the seeds.

The trail swings around an old well. The water here is *not* safe to drink.

Follow the moderate slope upward to the left. At .2 miles you reach a log lean-to with bunk area tucked up under its short front overhang. A stone fireplace highlights this cozy, primitive dwelling.

The path continues gradually to the top of Russell Hill, elevation 2,540 feet. It levels out and then descends a gentle slope past moss-covered glacial boulders. At .4 miles you look down into a ravine and begin the steep descent to its bottom.

Once there, the only way is up as you follow the blue blazes over the boulder-strewn hillside.

Cresting the slope leading up from the ravine, the trail becomes more gradual. It leads over, around, and between a long series of rocks and boulders. Many are covered with wavy broom moss.

The path crosses an old grassed-in road. It makes a short climb and then levels out through beech trees and more boulders.

Winding steadily but moderately upward, the path flattens out once again. For a surprisingly long way, it meanders over rock- and root-free ground.

A long, sloping upward climb reminds you that you are still heading for Shrewsbury Peak. Yellow birches appear to the left. Less striking than their white cousin, these trees have a creamy yellow or silver grey bark which peels in thin curls. Broken twigs give off a wintergreen odor.

A dry brook bed is crossed at 1.3 miles. A small cairn points the way as the trail bears right and begins a steeper climb.

Thick, low balsams and red spruces begin to line the trail amid towering white birches.

The balsam has long, flat, bright-green needles with two parallel silver stripes underneath. The red spruce has shorter needles which spiral closely around hairy twigs.

At approximately 1.4 miles you begin to see red blazes on some trees to the left of the trail. These denote the boundaries of the Calvin Coolidge State Forest, through which part of the Shrewsbury Trail travels. The double blue blazes on occasional trees indicate a sharp turn in the trail.

The path now becomes more cluttered with roots and rocks. It twists and turns its way through evergreen fragrance. Becoming steeper, the way begins its final ascent to the summit.

Thick evergreens brush your body as you climb up over larger rocks and moss-covered ledge. Winding up through a long evergreen tunnel, you pass two overlooks on the right with views to the south.

The 3,737-foot summit sits in a small, ledged clearing with a wide view to the south and east. Blue arrows on the rock point in two directions. (The trail can be followed for another 2 miles to a junction with the Long Trail.)

Shrewsbury Peak

Looking straight ahead (south-east) from the ledge you see the two-pronged summit of Mount Ascutney beyond the second ridge. New Hampshire mountains can be seen on the horizon. Just left (east) of Mount Ascutney is Mount Kearsarge, elevation 2,937 feet. Far to the right of Ascutney (south-southeast) is Monadnock Mountain, elevation 3,165 feet.

Swinging in a chain to the south are closer Vermont mountains. Smith Peak and Ingalls Hill lead up to dual-peaked Burnt Mountain. Beyond are Bear and Salt Ash Mountains.

Your return trip follows the same route back to your car.

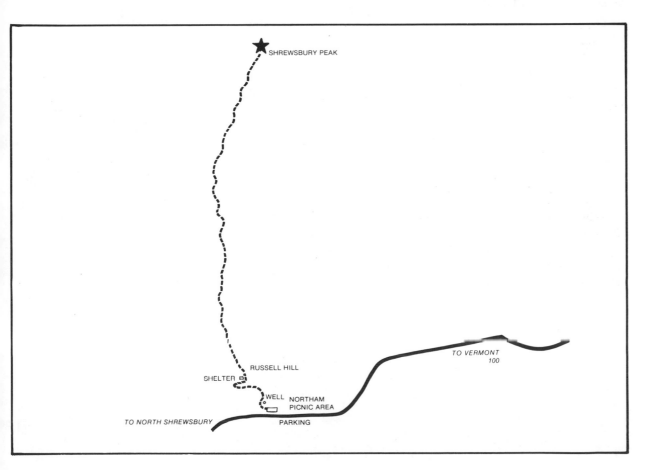

Shrewsbury Peak

At 4,241 feet, Killington is the second highest mountain in Vermont (only Mount Mansfield rises higher)—and certainly one of the most popular. It's a four-season peak, with teeming ski slopes in winter and lots of good hiking the rest of the year. And, always (weather permitting), the views are magnificent.

There are several ways to reach the top. For those who desire comfort, the gondola and main chairlift reach to within a short walk of the summit. But if you're more athletically inclined, the Bucklin Trail offers a nice combination of flat walking on old logging roads and steeper, more strenuous climbing over rocks

and inclines. The 6.8-mile round trip is long enough for a challenge yet short enough to allow plenty of time atop the mountain.

The trail begins at Brewers Corners on the Wheelerville Road. After you pass through Mendon on U.S. 4 going east, take the first right (after a cement road

Killington Peak

23. Killington Peak

Class: III
Elevation: 4,241 feet
Vertical rise: 2,531 feet
Distance (round trip): 6.8 miles
Hiking time: 4¼ hours

bridge) onto the green-signed Wheelerville Road. Follow it exactly 4 miles to a sharp bend to the right. This is Brewers Corners. The trail begins on the left just before the bend. The blue blazes and sign are just in off the road.

The old logging road passes along beneath towering pines, balsams, and spruces. The roar of water can be heard to the left as you leave the conifers and enter the hardwood forest.

Shortly ahead, you come to Brewers Brook. Cross it via the heavy wooden bridge which lists sharply to the right. The road begins a very gradual climb but continues to be easily walkable. The woods thin out as the hillsides slope upward above you to the right.

At .8 miles the road stops where the brook forms a Y. Cross to the middle, grassy area and follow it up to the left. Step carefully over this very rocky section.

About ¼ mile farther along, the path meets the slower flowing water and crosses over it. Blue blazes mark the way to the continu-

*View of summit
(Pico Peak beyond)*

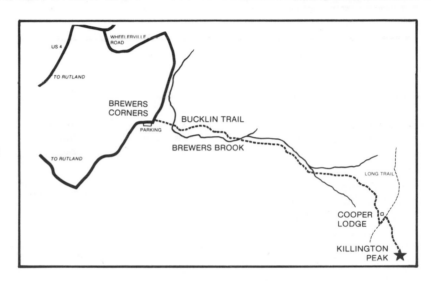

ation of the logging road on the other side.

Now on the north side of the brook, you quickly cross one of its small tributaries. The grade begins to increase slightly as goldenrod closes in from the sides.

At approximately 1.7 miles red markers cross the trail and stretch into the woods on both sides. These are the boundary markers for the Calvin Coolidge State Forest. Just beyond, the trail forks and the blue blazes lead you to the right.

The pleasantly flat logging road now gives way to moderate slopes strewn with loose rocks.

The trail narrows and winds upward through thin trees. Occasional openings to the left enable you to see towering companion peaks.

Winding upward to the right, the path becomes much greener along the edges. Hay-scented ferns swarm over the ground. Broom moss, wood sorrel, and shining club moss cluster around the bases of trees.

At approximately 2.3 miles the trail crosses an old grassed-in logging road. It continues upward through white birches, which are quickly replaced by evergreens.

The path flattens out a bit, be-

Killington Peak

fore swinging upward to the right through thick stands of conifers. Note that you have just left the north side of the ridge and are now climbing straight up the slope in a southerly direction.

Red osier dogwood brushes against your legs and fills a large clearing to the left.

This shrub is common throughout northern New England. Its branches spread loosely along the ground and rise no higher than six feet at the tips. The leaves are prominently veined, nearly smooth underneath, and pale. This shrub bears dark red branches in winter; small white flowers in flat-topped clusters in June.

At 3.2 miles you reach an intersection and go left toward (clearly visible) Cooper Lodge. The trail winds sharply right just before the lodge and joins the Long Trail South for approximately 100 feet, to a clearing. The Long Trail bears right here and you continue straight ahead up the .2 mile spur to Killington Peak.

Rocks and small boulders fill the blue-blazed trail as it veers right at a fork. A tumble of rocks and ledge makes the climbing more difficult. Hands become as useful as feet here. Passing upward through scrub growth, you reach the open-ledged summit.

The mountaintop is surprisingly, and disappointingly, civilized. A lookout tower and radio installation greet you first. On a short spur trail to the east is the Killington Gondola Terminal and Restaurant.

(In 1763 Rev. Sam Peters, a Connecticut clergyman, rode through central Vermont on a preaching and baptizing mission. He claimed to have christened the state "Verd-Mont," from the summit of Killington.)

From various points you can see to the distant horizons in all directions. Pico Peak rises to the immediate north. Green Mountain peaks are visible north to Mount Mansfield and south to Glastenbury Mountain. The city of Rutland nestles in a long valley to the west, and beyond are the Taconics, Lake Champlain, and the Adirondacks. Eastward the White Mountains can be seen, while Mount Ascutney is the only prominent peak to the southeast.

When ready, return to your car via the same trail.

Killington Peak

24. Deer Leap Mountain

Class: II & V
Elevation: 2,782 feet
Vertical rise: 680 feet
Distance (around loop): 2.7 miles
Hiking time: 2 hours

This climb should be viewed as two separate hikes. You'll make the loop tour of Deer Leap Mountain's two peaks and saddle over vastly different routes. The ascent via the Long Trail and Deer Leap Trail is gradual-to-moderate; the descent from Little Deer Leap (the southern peak) is precipitous. You'll use your hands often as you pick your way down over steep-ledged sections.

Start at the Long Trail North in Sherburne Pass. At the height-of-land on U.S. 4 between Rutland and Sherburne you will see the Long Trail Lodge. Just to the east a sign marks the Long and Appalachian trails. There is off-the-road parking on both sides of the highway here.

Climb 150 feet from the road to the fork where the Deer Leap and Long trails split. You are taking the gradual way up and the steeper way down. Keep right on the white-blazed Long Trail.

The trail winds along the side of the slope. Above and to the left, hundreds of large boulders crowd the slope. The path is littered with

Lower Lookout of Deer Leap Mountain

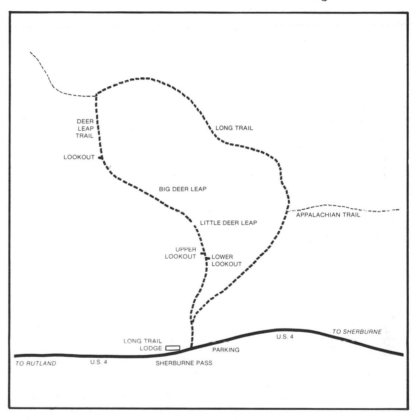

rocks and small boulders. Walk carefully.

Below to the right, U.S. 4 parallels the path. The loud motor vehicle noises remind you that you haven't yet escaped civilization.

The trail swings upward to the left and begins to slice along the east side of the slope. Huge masses of ledge jut out from the

hillside above and eventually crowd close to the path. Pass upward through a slender opening between these giants.

Roots and stones continue to make the walking rough as you climb moderately upward. The path becomes more gradual and the footing smoother, as you meander over short dips and rises.

Deer Leap Mountain

After roughly ½ mile the woods suddenly open before you. The sloping hillsides disappear, as you enter a flat clearing.

Many signs mark this important trail intersection. This is the junction of the Appalachian and Long trails. From here the Long Trail continues north to Canada, while the Appalachian swings east toward New Hampshire and its northern terminus on Mount Katahdin in Maine. Keep left on the Long Trail.

The path remains flat except for occasional bends around boulders. Becoming strewn with rocks, it swings gradually up to the left. It passes by a huge moss-covered boulder supporting an old birch tree. Roots cling to the stone surface like octopus' tentacles.

Thin, fragile-looking trees line the trail as it begins a very gradual, long, winding descent. At 1.2 miles the two trails rejoin. Follow the blue-blazed Deer Leap Trail as it turns sharply left.

Short spruces take over the left hillside as the trail passes briefly through a steeper section. The path becomes more gradual, as you wind through more young spruces. The grade becomes first more moderate, and then steep, before returning to its familiar gradual incline.

Some of the large tree trunks and stumps that line the way have hundreds of small, evenly-spaced holes girdling their bark. They were made by the yellow-bellied sapsucker. This bird makes the holes while eating the inner bark. He wisely returns later to eat both the sap and the insects that have been attracted to it.

Thick stands of spruce gather around the trail just before it passes through an area dense with ferns. Two large trees next to a huge boulder on the right mark a lookoff. Limited views to the northwest are available here.

The path winds upward and becomes steeper. It flattens out in an open area surrounded by ledge on the left. Passing through thick spruces, the path becomes spongy with needles. You soon reach a sign titled Deer Leap Height (just west of Big Deer Leap, the northern peak of Deer Leap Mountain). The elevation here is 2,770 feet.

The trails drops first moderately, then gradually, into the valley separating Deer Leap Mountain's two peaks. At 2.2 miles you come to a sign indicating it is about ½ mile to Sherburne Pass.

Cross a small brook and climb steeply up through white birches and under overhanging ledge. Walk along the ridge to the sign for Little Deer Leap, the southern peak of the mountain. The elevation here is 2,580 feet.

The path twists and turns through a spruce-lined area. Traffic sounds get louder as you begin to descend.

Soon you reach a huge mass of white, quartz-streaked ledge. This is the Upper Lookout. Climb up for striking views of Sherburne Pass and surrounding mountains.

One hundred feet below, you walk out onto the Lower Lookout. From this ledged area you look up to Pico Peak across Sherburne Pass and down to U.S. 4.

The remaining descent to your car is very steep. It slides down over smooth ledge and through jumbled sections of massive boulders. After stepping down a log ladder and using a nylon cable along a particularly steep section, you descend quickly to U.S. 4 and your car.

Deer Leap Mountain

25. Blue Ridge Mountain

Class: III
Elevation: 3,278 feet
Vertical rise: 1,487 feet
Distance (round trip): 4.8 miles
Hiking time: 2½ hours

A beautiful, cascading waterfall and hordes of yellow birches enrich the sides of the 2.4-mile-long Canty Trail. It takes you to Blue Ridge Mountain's summit, after a steep ascent through deciduous forests and a final meandering walk through evergreens. Once there, you get one of the best close views of the Coolidge Range. You can also look to the west beyond Rutland, to Bird and Herrick mountains with the Adirondacks on the horizon. On a clear day when the light is right, you can see what appears to be a misty field just east of the Adirondacks. This, of course, is Lake Champlain. Stratton and Dorset mountains lie to the south and southwest.

On U.S. 4 drive 6.1 miles from the junction of routes 4 and 7 in Rutland. Turn north onto Old Turnpike Road. Drive for .6 miles and turn left onto the second dirt road, which leads to Tall Timber Camping. Bear left at the fork and continue until you come to the large main building. Park your car in the field to the left.

Following the road, walk around to the right beyond this large

Cascade

Blue Ridge Mountain

brown building. Continue right at the fork here. You will quickly come to a number of signs. An arrow points the way to Blue Ridge.

Turn left into the woods and follow the blue blazes of the Canty Trail (which are, initially, paired with the green ones of the shorter, Green Trail).

A trail junction soon appears. The Canty Trail leaves the Green Trail behind, crosses the brook, and bears right. Very soon, you ford the brook again and resume a gradual walk.

The sides of the path are thickly forested with evergreens. After paralleling the brook, the trail crosses it once more, with the help of a log bridge at .3 miles.

There is still no noticeable gain in elevation as the way proceeds over a series of dips and rises. After crossing still another stream, you follow an old road for a short distance.

There is one more stream to cross at .6 miles before the trail begins a more serious climb toward the summit. Ascend the steep stream bank and follow the winding path. It turns right onto another old road which parallels

the brook below to the right.

The trail soon becomes more jumbled with rocks as the slope increases sharply. This is the steepest and most rugged section of the entire Canty Trail. Closer to the summit the path resumes its gradual, meandering ways.

There are large-tooth aspen along the pathside here. These northeastern trees somewhat resemble the trembling aspen, but have heavier twigs and larger, coarser leaves. The round-toothed, heart-shaped leaves are their most

distinctive characteristic. The soft, light wood is used for pulp, excelsior, boxes, and matches.

After approximately 1½ miles, rushing white water catches your eye below to the right. You might want to make your way down through the woods for a closer look. The cascading water slides over smooth ledge and narrows to slither around outcroppings in the rock. It swirls into tranquil pools before tumbling downward again.

Paralleling the water, the path follows an old washed-out road.

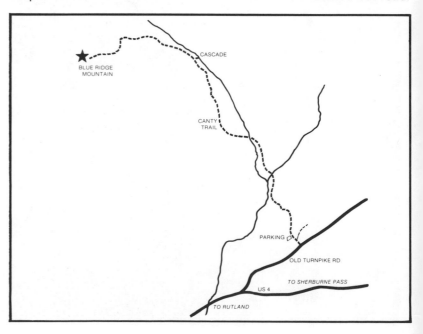

Blue Ridge Mountain

The higher sides offer more solid footing than the rutted, rockied middle.

Yellow birches have been the most prominent tree along the way. These trees display silver-yellow bark, and may grow as high as one hundred feet. Their double-toothed oval leaves have a wintergreen fragrance. Stands of these trees are a sign of rich, well-drained soil.

Continuing upward, the path becomes much more gradual. Shining club moss gathers its glossy spires together to form sparkling green patches at the base of tree trunks.

Evergreen spills cushion your walking as the trail brushes between spruces and balsams. The deliciously pungent fragrance of balsam fills your nostrils.

After meandering upward to the left, the path suddenly swings right at 2.3 miles.

Scramble over some ledge and enter the clearing at the summit. Above to the right are large rocks which serve as vantage points. They will enable you to see in all possible directions. Return to your car by the same route.

Along the Canty Trail

Blue Ridge Mountain

Quechee Gorge

Quechee Gorge, Vermont's "Little Grand Canyon," was carved out through the ages by the waters of the Ottauquechee River.

In the middle 1800s the gorge and a nearby area with a steep grade impeded construction of the Woodstock Railroad, planned to link White River Junction and Rutland. Finally, in 1875, twenty-eight years after the Woodstock R.R. was originally chartered, ways were found to overcome these two natural barriers. Passengers were enlisted to help push the train cars up the incline. The gorge was spanned by a two hundred and eighty-two-foot trestle, crossing one hundred and sixty-five feet above the river.

For years the Woodstock Railroad trestle was the highest railroad bridge in New England. Now remodeled, it is presently used as the U.S. 4 highway bridge, crossing the gorge six miles east of Woodstock and five miles west of White River Junction.

The view from the route 4 bridge can be easily reached by car, but it will be far more rewarding after a walk along the Quechee Gorge Trail.

On route 4, .3 miles east of the

Quechee Gorge

28. Quechee Gorge

Class: II
Elevation: 640 feet
Vertical rise: 125 feet
Distance (to bridge above gorge and back): 1.5 miles
Hiking time: 1 hour

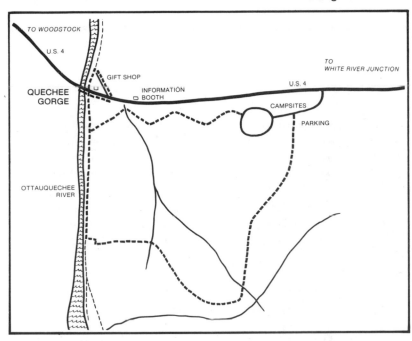

gorge, you will see the Quechee State Park entrance sign. Turn into the entrance on the south side of the road and proceed along the dirt road for .2 miles. Park your car at the small area on the right near a "Firewood" sign. Cross to the firewood area on the left of the road. At the rear of this clearing is a sign for Quechee Gorge Trail. Blue blazes mark the way.

A delicious pine odor engulfs you momentarily as you approach the trail, but disappears quickly as white pines are replaced by hemlocks. Tiny cones and red-brown needles blanket the meandering woodland trail. The path is flat and cushiony underfoot.

At approximately ¼ mile the trail veers sharply to the right and descends a steep grade through stands of white birch and hemlock. This descent terminates in a small gully at the .3-mile mark.

After leading up out of the gulley, the trail drops to a small brook.

The water's whispery gurgle interrupts the quiet of the glen. Roots traversing the trail form natural steps down to the water. Cross the brook on logs furry with moss.

Beyond the stream the path rises steeply once again and bears sharply to the right at the top of the grade.

At approximately ½ mile, the path crosses a medium-sized stream tumbling from right to left. The trail climbs a small embankment beyond the stream and levels out once again. The way is mirey, and confettied with pine needles.

Soon the trail joins an old, narrow grassy road and makes a 90-degree turn to the left.

After only a few steps, the din of the Ottauquechee coursing through the gorge can be heard. After another 100 yards the road emerges from the wood and abuts an even wider road paralleling the gorge.

Directly across this road you can pause at an overlook. Here the Ottauquechee is dwarfed by the sides of the chasm stretching high above.

After viewing the gorge from this vantage point, return to

the road and go left. At the ¾-mile mark you begin a long climb to the U.S. 4 bridge.

Cresting the hill, with the bridge in sight ahead, note the blue trail marker leading sharply into the woods on the right. This will be your return route. Continue straight, however, for a look at the gorge from the top. The way passes under the bridge and shortly thereafter follows a reverse 45-degree angle (right) up to route 4.

Peering into the gorge on the north side can give you a dizzy feeling. Hemlock, pine, and maple grip the sides of this jagged slashway and funnel your gaze downward. The Ottauquechee River courses lava-like along the bottom of this deep cleft. Stretches of fast water scratch its dark surface with white.

Cross the bridge to the other side. The gorge appears much straighter and narrower here. The river moves faster and has molded deep impressions into the rocks.

Retrace your steps on route 4, around the gift shop, and back down under the bridge. Watch for the blue marker on your left.

The trail eases back into the deeper woods and meanders parallel to and below route 4. The quiet softness of the forest is shattered intermittently by the droning of automobiles above.

Pass over a small stream with assistance from fallen logs and immediately turn right past a massive dead, barkless tree. Follow the path beside the water.

Two hundred yards after crossing the brook the trail runs into a wider path at a 90-degree angle. Follow the blue markers and the arrow pointing left. The path bears gradually around to the right and unexpectedly leads onto a narrower way at a 45-degree angle. Go right here. Be alert; it is easy to miss this turn.

The trail becomes quite steep as it climbs up to the circular camping road at campsite #15. Go left past the rest rooms and Quechee State Park bulletin board. You may now either continue a short distance along the road or take the little path straight across an open field to your car.

Quechee Gorge

27. Amity Pond Natural Area

Class: II
Elevation: 1,650 feet
Vertical rise: 660 feet
Distance (around the area): 2.6 miles
Hiking time: 1¾ hours

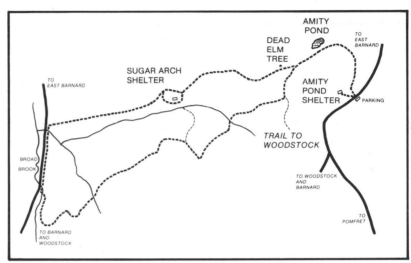

In 1969, Elizabeth and Richard Brett deeded this land to the state of Vermont to be used for hiking, snowshoeing, cross country skiing, and horseback riding. No motor vehicles are allowed here. Even radios are prohibited. The Amity Pond Natural Area is a place to refresh your senses and spirit.

Fires are permitted only at the shelters. Hikers are asked to remain on the trails to avoid any possible damage to the area. Picking or cutting flowers, plants, or trees are also disallowed.

From Woodstock drive north on Vt. 12 for 1.2 miles. As the road forks, bear right toward South Pomfret. Stay on this road for 2 miles to another fork at the South Pomfret Post Office. Go right toward Pomfret. Drive for 4.7 miles on this road and go left onto the paved road just after the wide bend to the right. After .3 miles go left at another fork onto a dirt road. Drive 2.2 miles and watch for the entrance to the Amity Pond Natural Area.

The absence of large signs is in keeping with the area's philoso-

Amity Pond

phy. Watch carefully for the blue and orange diamond-shaped trail marker and a poster sign on a tree to the left of the road. There is limited parking across the road from the entrance.

Pass through the narrow opening in the barbed-wire fence into a field dotted with young red pine. Almost immediately after the trail begins, a short spur leads left to the rustic Amity Pond Shelter. The shelter faces a temporary pond, which is part of a water conservation experiment.

Return to the main trail and follow its wide, flat grassy path. The blue and orange diamonds guide you along.

To the right of the height-of-land is Amity Pond itself, bounded by a small area of ledge, shrubs, tall grass, and reeds. You can look to the south from here and see the saddle-backed hump of Mount Ascutney. The view to the west takes in the high pointed top of Killington Peak and the cone-shaped summit of Pico Peak.

An interesting tale describes how the pond got its name. Two girls who attended the East Barnard school together became chums and promised each other "friendship forever." When one married a man from the town of Pomfret and the other wed a man from Barnard, it was difficult for them

Amity Pond Natural Area

to get together. So, by mail, they arranged to share a basket lunch on specified days at the grassy hill beside this tiny pond, which thus became known as Amity Pond.

The wide, flat trail winds down through the large, open meadow. Tall grasses, goldenrod, and milkweed brush your legs. Ahead is a single large dead elm tree. The path branches toward the elm and keeps just left of it. It then makes a wide arc to the right toward the far corner of the meadow. Passing between sections of an old stone wall, the trail enters the hardwood forest.

The wide, flat, easily-walkable trail bends to the right and meanders gradually down through the woods. After .6 miles you enter a small meadow where a spur leads left to the Sugar Arch Shelter.

Now grassy, the way passes beneath power lines and continues steadily downward. Thick stands of hemlock and occasional pines and spruces line the trail as a small brook parallels it to the left.

Just short of the 1-mile mark you step out into a huge open field. To the right are a church and cemetery; to the left, a farm house. Make your way across the open area to the road straight ahead.

Turn left onto the road and walk past a second farmhouse on the left. Just beyond, you cross the cement-sided road bridge over Broad Brook. Approximately 60 feet after the bridge the trail leads left off the road. It drops down through shrubbery to a trail sign and the brook.

Be alert for animal signs along the water and in damp areas ahead. A raccoon's imprint is particularly distinctive. Its front and hind feet have a pad with five slender toes. The tracks are usually paired with the left hind foot placed beside the right fore foot.

Rock hop across Broad Brook and continue up into the woods (ignore the short spur to the left just after the brook). Evergreens canopy the trail as the orange and blue markers lead you beside the brook for a short distance.

Swing left and climb the moderate grade beside a barbed-wire fence. After a series of upward twists and turns, the path crosses a small stream via slim, cut logs.

After 2 miles a trail joins from the left. Continue straight here.

A stone wall parallels the trail as you climb steadily upward. The path flattens out and passes beneath power lines. It then drops down a moderate grade to the bottom of a narrow gully and crosses over a trickling brook at 2.2 miles.

Beyond the brook you ascend a steep incline to the right. Near the top of this open-wooded slope you enter a small, round clearing. The trail swings sharply left, and climbs to the top of a hill lined by a sparkling stand of white birches.

Cresting this rise, you step out into the southwestern corner of the meadow where Amity Pond is located. In the distance to the left is the old dead elm. Follow the orange and blue markers to the trail junction just below the height-of-land beside Amity Pond. Continue past the pond and follow the path back to your car.

28. Mount Carmel

Class: III
Elevation: 3,365 feet
Vertical rise: 1,598 feet
Distance (round trip): 4.4 miles
Hiking time: 2½ hours

Artist's Fungus

Mount Carmel's summit tower makes available a full circle of glorious views. The open platform looks south across picturesque Chittenden Reservoir to Blue Ridge Mountain and the Coolidge Range. In the opposite direction, Green Mountain peaks curve slowly northward. The Adirondacks and White Mountains fill the distant horizons to the west and east respectively.

The first part of this hike follows the New Boston Trail. To reach its beginning, drive north on Mountain Top Road from the military memorial statue in the town of Chittenden. After 1.7 miles bear right onto the gravel road at the fork just beyond the Mountain Top Inn. This extremely rough road continues 1.4 miles to a brown-and-white sign on the left marking the start of the New

Boston Trail. Park well off the road here.

For the first 1¼ miles the blue blazes of this path follow a jeep trail. Much of this section is a pleasant walk, with only slight increases in elevation. The ruggedest hiking and the most rapid rise in elevation occur during the final .3 miles to the summit.

The trail begins by following an

old road left through a field. It enters the woods and passes between and beneath spire-like spruces. After approximately ¼ mile the road forks. Bear left here.

The pitch increases as you reach a second fork shortly ahead. Take the right road here. On both sides of the trail, rotting oak and beech stumps display bracketed growths of artist's fungus (so named for the pictures craftsmen like to paint on their smooth white undersides). Shades of brown and tan color the smoothly rippled sections of their upper surfaces.

Easy walking through beech-filled forests brings you to the third trail fork after ¾ miles. Follow the blue blazes to the left here. After more gentle dips and rises you cross over a small stream.

The red blazes of the Mount Carmel State Forest cross the path at 1.4 miles. Just beyond is Carmel Camp and the end of the jeep trail. Residents of Proctor maintain this steel building for their own use during deer season, but permit hikers to use it the rest of the year. A spring bubbles a bit north on the New Boston Trail.

Follow the winding, blue-blazed foot trail to the left of Carmel Camp. The packed dirt path swings upward to the right and reaches the Long Trail at 1.7 miles.

Turn left onto the Long Trail and follow its white blazes north. This steady upward grade arrives at the sign for the Mount Carmel Trail at 1.9 miles. Go right onto this unblazed but well-trodden path.

The way swings around to the left through bunches of hobblebush. Its leaves are large (four-to-eight inches), nearly round, finely-toothed, and heart-shaped at the base. In winter, distinctive buds will help you recognize this shrub: two small leaves enclose a tiny flower at the twig ends. These twigs and buds are favored by deer for winter browsing.

The path twists and turns up Mount Carmel's south slope. You really have to lean into this steep ascent. After entering a small clearing covered with spruce and balsam spills, the way climbs straight up to the summit.

Atop the tower, near views include 3,485-foot Bloodroot Mountain to the north-northwest, 3,342-foot Round Mountain to the north-northeast, and 2,753-foot Mount Nickawaket almost due west.

Follow the same route back to your car.

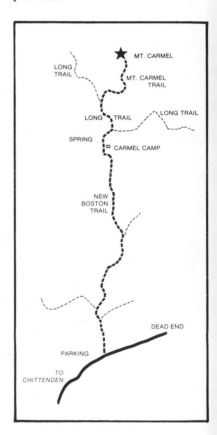

29. Abbey Pond

Class: II
Elevation: 1,700 feet
Vertical rise: 1,250 feet
Distance (round trip): 3.4 miles
Hiking time: 2¼ hours

You will be touched by Abbey Pond's primitiveness and tranquility. An early morning or late afternoon visit to the pond might acquaint you with some of its more bashful neighbors. The masked nocturnal raccoon may leave his long-fingered pawprints, after feeding on frogs and crayfish. Deer come to drink and browse on pondside shrubbery. Muskrats nest along the sides of the pond and sometimes build above-water homes like those of the beaver.

Drive north on U.S. 7 into Middlebury. Pass the Addison County Court House and take the next right. At the stop sign bear right onto Seminary Street Extension. Bear left at the fork after 1.4 miles onto Quarry Road. Follow it to the end where it meets Vt. 116 (Case Street) and turn left (north).

After .7 miles turn east onto a dirt road. The road divides immediately. Take the right fork and follow the dark blue blazes on the trees.

Approximately .4 miles after turning onto the dirt road you'll reach an intersection. Straight

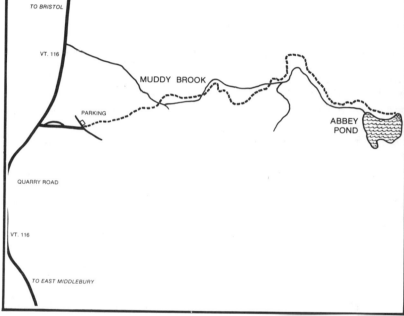

ahead, blue blazes and a small blue arrow mark the start of the trail. Pull your car well off the road to avoid interfering with gravel trucks.

Follow the blue blazes along an old logging road. The way is wide and gradual. Some rocks dot the path, but are easily avoided.

Giant glacial boulders, many with trees and mosses flourishing atop their great masses, appear to the right.

The pitch increases. Swinging

left, the dirt path passes below moss-covered ledge. After approximately ¼ mile you cross over fast-flowing Muddy Brook, which finds its source in Abbey Pond. To the right a twenty-five-foot waterfall spills down into a series of small pools.

Soon the trail swings right and begins to parallel the brook, whose muffled rushing will accompany you for some time.

At .6 miles the brook again passes beneath the trail. Bearing left, the path maintains a steady upward incline. The brook courses along the bottom of the ravine below.

At 1.1 miles the now more gradual trail passes over a black boggy area and crosses a gentler section of the brook via narrow logs. Beyond the brook the path wanders over and around small rocks. It remains flat, with only minimal dips and rises, the rest of the way to the pond.

Winding along a spongier trail through thick woods, you arrive at Abbey Pond. Two small peaks rise above, and reflect down into, its waters.

Looking around the pond you'll see a beaver dam at the near end.

Look down the pond to the dead trees rising at the other end and you'll see the lodge itself.

Sit quietly on a sun-warmed rock near the water's edge; watch and listen. A salamander may be scuttling along the bottom. These tailed amphibians eat insects, worms, and other small invertebrates. In early summer, their eggs are found in jelly-like clusters in the shallows.

The pond is a haven for ducks and geese. Metal and wooden boxes near the beaver lodge serve as nesting sites for the multi-colored wood duck. Abbey Pond's shallowness and its aquatic plants attract other surface-

feeding ducks such as mallards and blacks. You may see them "tipping up" as they eat off the lush bottom.

The belted kingfisher also lives here. He has distinctive blue-grey markings, a white throat band, large bill, and a crested head. He flies erratically, yet can hover suspended over the water before plunging in for small fish.

Trout create circles of ripples as they surface for food. They often leap completely out of the water in their pursuit of insects.

Return to your car filled with some of the quiet of this woodland pond.

"The pond"

Abbey Pond

30. Mount Abraham

Class: III
Elevation: 4,052 feet
Vertical rise: 1,642 feet
Distance (round trip): 5 miles
Hiking time: 3½ hours

One of the more popular day hikes, as well as a favorite with overnighters on the Long Trail, is Mount Abraham. Its easy access and striking views (one of the most far-reaching panoramas on the entire Long Trail) make it a very desirable climb.

Early settlers called Mount Abraham "Potatoe Hill" because of its resemblance to an oversized, well-banked potato mound. This name was not completely accepted, however, and map publishers changed it to Lincoln Mountain—for the Revolutionary War figure General Benjamin Lincoln. When Colonel Joseph Battell bought the mountain in the late 1800s (as part of his plan for conserving Vermont forests), he renamed it Mount Abraham, after our sixteenth president. He then named the neighboring mountain to the north Lincoln Peak.

From either Lincoln or Warren, drive along the Lincoln-Warren Highway to the top of Lincoln Gap. Cresting the highest point of land, you'll see the brown and yellow sign for the Long Trail and Green Mountain National Forest. There is ample parking here both off and along the road,

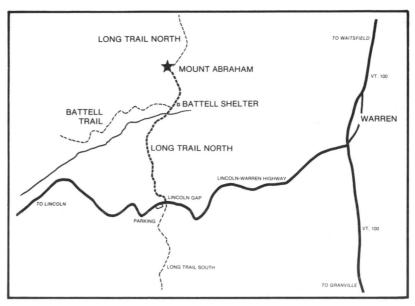

but on a clear weekend day you might arrive to find the roadside already packed with vehicles of all kinds.

Ascend the short, steep embankment on the north side of the highway. At its crest, the trail forks. Stay left along the sharply sloping hillside. The path narrows as it passes behind slender young birches. White blazes guide you right, and gradually upward.

Surprisingly, there are a number of abrupt descents during this first half of your trek up Mount Abraham. The trail swings sharply

left, then right, as it drops down over rooted steps. Dipping steadily, it switches back sharply right and winds past a long series of moss-covered ledges.

The smoothness of the path yields to rocks as the way passes upward through snowy birches. A small section of ledge insures a gradual rise. Once on top, you gaze down a short, steep dropoff. Serpentine roots cling to the ledge, providing sure footing.

Moving gradually upward, you come to red blazes flanking and crossing the trail. These mark the

Mount Abraham

boundary of the Green Mountain National Forest.

Two huge boulders squeeze the trail at the 1.2-mile mark. (They are called "the Carpenters" after two trail workers so named.) Old stumps, rotted into a variety of poses, dot the way.

The 2,410-foot base elevation at Lincoln Gap is responsible for the fact that the gap is closed in winter, and for the lack of traditional hardwood forests along this trail. Instead, the trailsides teem with fluffy young spruce and balsam. They are so closely packed that you wonder how they will survive. Stately older trees rise above these younger ones.

An opening in the thick trees suddenly appears. Straight ahead you can see the massive dome of Mount Abraham. Tree-covered except for the actual summit, it appears quite imposing from this distance. You are now roughly one mile from the top.

A trickling brook crosses the trail. It offers cool, refreshing water, and a good excuse to rest. Just ahead, the Battell Trail joins from the left. Battell Shelter is 250 yards upward to the right. A sturdy, smooth-sided shelter, it can sleep six to eight hikers. Spring water is available 100 feet to the east.

From the shelter, the trail changes little as it climbs to the top. Thick stands of spruce and balsam create a cloistered atmosphere. Twists and turns over intermittent stretches of ledge necessitate careful stepping.

Approaching the summit amid dwarfed scrub growth, the trail confronts an unusually beautiful boulder. White, veined with black, the giant piece of quartz is surely a rarity. Against the drab grey-greens of the ledge and spruce, it stands out strikingly.

Reaching the summit, you see several circles of piled rocks. Looking like the bottoms of unfinished stone igloos, these barriers offer protection from blustery winds.

The views are superb. You can look west across Lake Champlain and clearly see the Adirondacks, with Mount Marcy most prominent. Southward, Green Mountain peaks stretch as far as Killington. Mount Ascutney looms on the horizon to the southeast. Mounts Lafayette and Washington are in the distant east. Looking north, you can follow a panoramic profile from the distinctive Camel's Hump, past Mount Mansfield, up to Jay Peak and Belvidere Mountain.

The Warren-Sugarbush Airport (a local center for soaring enthusiasts) is below and to the east. You can become mesmerized by the gliders if you're on Mount Abraham when the weather is clear and the winds are right. Sunlight glitters off gliders' wings, as they drift lazily earthward.

Return to reality; your car awaits 2.5 miles below at Lincoln Gap.

Massive quartz rock near summit

Mount Abraham

Hikers nearing Mt. Abraham's summit

Mount Abraham

Trail to Mount Ellen

Mount Ellen

31. Mount Ellen

Class: IV
Elevation: 4,083 feet
Vertical rise: 2,508 feet
Distance (round trip): 8.2 miles
Hiking time: 6 hours

The view from Mount Ellen's wooded summit is not worth the 8.2-mile round-trip hike. But the challenge of steep, rugged trails over continuous inclines makes the climb exciting.

Mount Ellen shares with Camel's Hump the honor of being Vermont's third highest peak. Only Killington and Mansfield rise higher. This mountain is not as close to access roads as the others, however—so the trails to its summit are longer.

The climb leads steadily uphill almost all the way. Though it is gradual at times, you always are leaning into the path's relentless incline. Prepare for a long day's hiking.

From the junction of Vt. 17 and Vt. 116 northeast of Bristol, go east on route 17. Follow it 3.2 miles to the signed road leading to Jerusalem. Go right and travel 1.2 miles to the wooden signpost at the corner of a road leading left. Among the signs are ones for Chicken Lake and Jerusalem Trail (your route for the beginning of this hike). Go left .3 miles to the parking area at the edge of a field, again on the left (a house with large windows sits across the road).

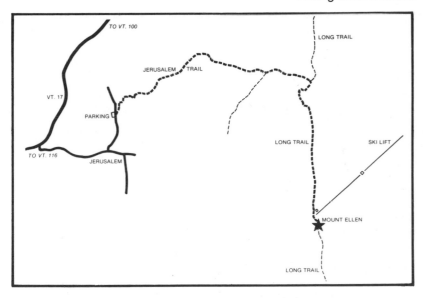

Walk left along the dirt road from the parking area. After a few hundred yards you will reach the start of the Jerusalem Trail. Follow the blue blazes into the woods and across a stream to the right.

Long, straight stretches, steady, inclines, and slim trees characterize the first mile. At .8 miles the path swings left and begins its steepest climb so far. A blue-blazed boulder, entrenched in the middle of the trail, marks the spot.

Thick stands of maples fill the forest as the grade maintains its upward trend. Both black and sugar maples grow here. (Black maple sap, too, is used to produce the famous Vermont maple syrup.) These two types of maples are distinguishable by their leaves. The black maple's are three-lobed with shallow notches and drooping edges. The sugar maple's are five-lobed with moderately deep notches and firm edges.

At 1.2 miles the path bears right and changes direction from east to south. The high ridge line of the Green Mountain chain now becomes visible above to the left.

Mount Ellen

Dense thickets of hobblebush edge the path as it narrows and steepens. This straggling shrub is common throughout northern New England. The clustered, five-petaled, white flowers appear in May and June. The fruit (non-poisonous, but acidic) begins to develop in August, and changes from red to black at maturity.

The trail climbs a short, steep slope before weaving between stands of thin white birches.

An old grassy road joins the path from the right at 1.7 miles. The way becomes refreshingly gradual in places before it crosses two brooks, after which it resumes its steep way.

The easy walking has ended. For the next ½ mile the way leads very steeply upward. Rocks, ledge, and roots make the climbing more difficult.

At 2.3 miles the Jerusalem and Long trails meet. From here it is 1.8 miles to Mount Ellen. Turn right onto the Long Trail South.

This section south to Mount Ellen is quite typical of the Long Trail as it winds along ridges of the Green Mountains. It dips and rises while crossing from one side of the ridge line to the other. The footing ranges from rocky and rooty to boggy.

The rough trail descends gradually into a gully. Rising out, it passes through an area covered with many shades of green growth. Moss begins around tree trunks above the path and sweeps down over vertical ledge faces to the edge of the trail itself. Tree-filtered sunbeams highlight the rainbow of greenery.

Mount Ellen can be seen rising ahead as the way continues through lush, damp areas. Rocks and dead logs are choked by a variety of plant life. Wood sorrel, wavy broom moss, and blister and reindeer lichen exist side by side.

At 3.1 miles the path climbs over rocks and roots and begins a steady ascent to the summit. Dampness makes the trail slippery in spots.

A ski slope suddenly appears through the trees and parallels the trail just before you reach the northern boundary of the Green Mountain National Forest at 3.6 miles. At 3.9 miles a slide of loose rocks amid scrub evergreens provides a good stopping point. Wide views to the west are available here. The Adirondacks appear like giants on the not-too-distant horizon.

More ski trails slice through the forest. Continue through the trees to the upper station of the Glen Ellen Chair Lift. Look left down the slope for a view north to Camel's Hump and Mount Mansfield. Cross under the chair lift to the other side of the ski slope for a look to the east. Mount Alice, Bald, and Scrag mountains are to the northeast. Southeast: the peaks of Mount Cushman, Mount Olympus, and Rochester Mountain. New Hampshire summits form the distant backdrop.

Follow the white blazes past the end of the chair lift and up the short slope to the wooded summit.

Find a spot in the sun to warm yourself and rest in preparation for the return trip.

Sharp-leaved Wood Asters

Mount Ellen

Mount Ellen

Along the trail to Scrag Mountain

The most beautiful white-birch forests we've seen can be found in the cool woods on the slopes of Scrag Mountain.

To climb the trail through these handsome trees, drive to Waitsfield on Vt. 100. Turn southeast off Vt. 100 at the Jilson Public Library (the yellow-painted brick building). Drive .4 miles through a covered bridge to a fork in the road. Take the left fork and follow this road over a narrow bridge and up a steep hill for about ¾ miles. Turn right onto a gravel road which joins a four-way intersection after .7 miles. Go straight across, and continue for still another .7 miles. At this point there is a small parking area on the left—the last available parking before the road becomes impassable for cars.

Walk up the grade .4 miles to the fork. A sign for "Lookout Tower" points to the right. As you walk in this direction, your way is occasionally paralleled by low stone walls on either side of the road. Further along, hemlocks form a natural boundary.

Six-tenths of a mile from the parking area the way forks to both sides of a large hemlock. Follow the "Lookout Tower" sign to the left. The trail angles through dense patches of ferns and into thicker woods. It is still a crude road at this point, quite bumpy and rocky.

A few minutes of walking brings you to a clear stream. This is the last certain water on the trail to the summit. Pause here to refresh and prepare yourself for the climb ahead.

After the stream, the trail scrambles up over rocks, roots, and boulders. Young maples and beeches crowd the way. Though not excessively steep, the pitch of the upward grade is continually challenging.

An especially interesting large rock obstructs this lower part of the trail. Its surface is colored

Scrag Mountain

32. Scrag Mountain

Class: III
Elevation: 2,911 feet
Vertical rise: 1,491 feet
Distance (round trip): 4.2 miles
Hiking time: 3 hours

several shades of brown and pocketed with rounded depressions. Furry moss softens its face.

Scattered, solitary trees herald your approach to the promised assembly of white birches. They'll light your way for one-third of the hike to the tower.

Pick your way across dried stream beds, over the three-log bridge crossing a small gully, and then around the numerous rocks which have spilled down the trail.

As you climb higher, spruces join, and finally replace, the white birches.

After 1.8 miles of hiking, the trail divides. A sign indicates that the short trail straight ahead will lead to good water at the first stream or the second well. Another sign points left toward the Lookout Tower. Follow this left switchback .3 miles to the summit.

As you move along this trail, look through the trees to the left for a glimpse of blue mountain silhouettes. The path winds over alternately rising and level areas as it swings widely right. Climb past a brown hut into a small clearing. Limited views of various mountains, including the

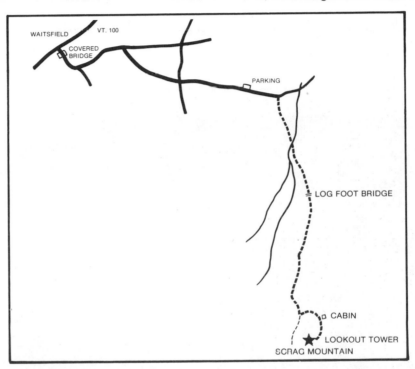

Lincoln Range, may be enjoyed from here.

For an opportunity to experience an extended circle of mountain views, continue along the trail to the Lookout Tower. You'll climb up over ledge on this last stretch of trail.

Camel's Hump and Mount Mansfield figure more prominently along the northwestern horizon. The Lincoln Range lines the west; south to north its peaks are:

Mount Abraham, Lincoln Peak, Nancy Hanks Peak, Cutts Peak, and Mount Ellen. To the southwest you'll see the Presidential Range (not to be confused with the similarly named range in New Hampshire). Looking east: Butterfield, Spruce, and Signal mountains. Mount Hunger, Mount Worcester, and White Rock Mountain are to the north.

When ready, return by the same route.

Scrag Mountain

*View of Smuggler's Notch from Bear
Pond Trail (Mount Mansfield)*

Northern Vermont

View of Spruce Mountain

Spruce Mountain lets you "get back to nature" in the purest sense. No ski trails, summit roads, or other encroachments of modern man scar its slopes. Its nearly twenty-five hundred acres comprise one of the most remote mountain tracts remaining in the entire state.

The land also contains one of Vermont's best wildlife habitats. Black bear breed here, as do numerous other woodland creatures. A recent Spruce Mountain ornithological study recorded sightings of seventy different birds.

The natural balance on Spruce Mountain has not yet been disturbed. But many of Vermont's unspoiled areas *have* been disappearing rapidly: sold to builders, developers, and speculators who care more for money than for the land. If we are to enjoy the peace, quiet, and exhilaration of communing with nature, this area—and others like it—must remain "wild."

The road to Spruce Mountain is located 4¼ miles south of Plainfield. Take the single road leading south from the center of town. Bear left at the first fork. Continue straight on this road to another fork. Go right here, following a sign to East Hill. Do not take the road to the left just after crossing a small road bridge. Take the next left onto Spruce Mountain Road.

Spruce Mountain

33. Spruce Mountain

Class: III
Elevation: 3,037 feet
Vertical rise: 1,177 feet
Distance (round trip): 3.9 miles
Hiking time: 3 hours

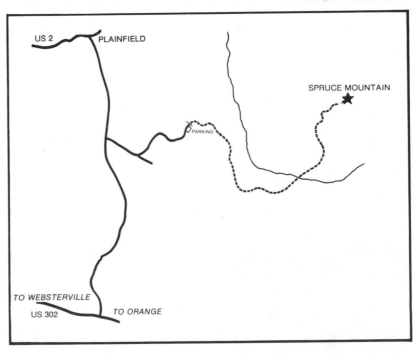

This road eventually swings left, with a narrow offshoot going right. Keep left here. Becoming very rocky and rutted, the way leads to an iron swing gate where there is ample parking on both sides. Should you be unable to reach this point by car, park at any of the widened areas along the way and walk the short distance to the gate.

Signs at the gate indicate the road is closed to vehicles but that hikers are welcome. Red blazes to the right and left of the barrier mark the boundary of Jones State Forest. A further sign guides you right toward the fire tower on the summit.

This initial section of trail is a wide, smooth road with a deep rut along the right side. As it crests a small knoll and begins a downward run, you can see the Spruce Mountain fire tower high in the distance to the left.

The way becomes increasingly grassy as it leads gradually upward. The mountain's outline occasionally is visible through trees to the left as the road continues its gradual climb. After approximately 1 mile the way narrows to trail width. The grassy path fills with stones, as you swing left and enter dense woods. Several damp, muddied patches lie ahead.

Stepping gingerly from rock to rock, you make your way to a log bridge that crosses a slow-moving brook. Beyond, the trail widens somewhat and becomes softer underfoot—although rocks continue to speckle the way. Walking becomes slower at times as you negotiate the bumpy footing.

Veering left, the path climbs moderately. Spruce and balsam line the trail as it steepens even more.

Passing steeply upward, the trail approaches two huge, looming glacial boulders at the 1.3-mile mark. Short spruces grow atop them, appearing to be anchored by only a thick carpet of moss. The trail swings left in front of these gargantuan guards and begins a passage over sloping ledge.

Scraggy old spruces and balsams stand watch over smaller,

bushy ones as the trail climbs more steeply. It seems impossible that the closely bunched young trees can find room to grow. .

The path passes over long sections of beautiful white-with-black-flecked granite ledge as it winds upward.

Roots slither across the trail as it begins its final push to the top. The way suddenly levels out. It becomes a gradual dirt path lined with grass and ferns. The abbreviated height of the trees, combined with the low grass and shrubs at the trail sides, creates an open, airy atmosphere.

The fire tower can be seen ahead, as you pass more slabs of granite ledge. It is one of only five still in operation in the entire state. A watchman lives in the little cabin beyond it from April through October. He is the last of a fast-dying breed; planes have virtually monopolized surveillance duties.

The views from the tower are spectacular. On a clear day you can see west across Lake Champlain to Adirondack peaks eighty miles away. Mount Washington's summit is visible seventy-five miles to the east. Numerous Vermont peaks can be seen within these perimeters.

Return to your car by the same route.

Spruce Mountain

34. Osmore Pond and Little Deer Mountain

Class: II
Elevation: 1,760 feet
Vertical rise: 660 feet
Distance (to pond, mountain, and back): 5.2 miles
Hiking time: 3½ hours

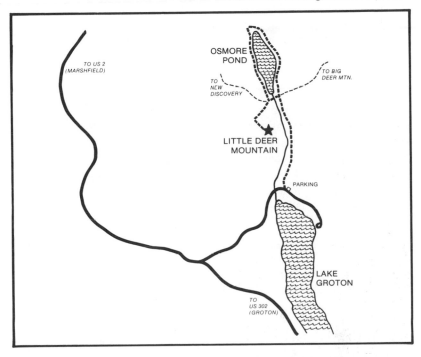

More than twenty thousand acres of land lie within the boundaries of Groton State Forest, making it the largest single unit of state-owned land in Vermont. Numerous game animals, especially deer, thrive here. Groton's spruce-fir swamps are a prime area for winter deer yarding.

Trails marked with blue paint are for hikers and snowshowers only. Those indicated by orange reflectorized diamonds are "multipurpose" (all-terrain vehicles excluded).

People come to Groton State Forest for many reasons: they picnic, swim, camp, cook, hunt, go fishing and boating, enjoy the scenery, and mob the refreshment stand. When we're there, we like to visit Osmore Pond and climb Little Deer Mountain. The walk to the pond is pleasantly undemanding; the hike up Little Deer, moderately strenuous.

Groton State Forest is located on the road which connects U.S 302 west of Groton and U.S. 2 east of Marshfield. Drive from either end to the green and yellow sign listing Groton State Forest, Big Deer, and Stillwater. Turn in here and go straight for 1.3 miles. You will see brown and

View across Osmore Pond to Little Deer Mountain

white signs for Osmore and New Discovery on the left. There is limited parking off the road just past the trail.

Follow the path as it leads into the woods just to the right of the signs. The blue blazes and orange reflectorized diamonds mark this section as a multi-purpose trail.

Sides of the trail overflow with fern growth. This gives the open woods a softly-feathered look. It accents the startling white-

ness of paper birches and shiny creaminess of yellow birches.

The trail parallels a merrily flowing brook, occasionally dipping down near it. As it begins to climb gradually, the path swings away from the brook. Moving through the shadows of a stand of spruce, you can hear the wind brush the tree tops. Behind and below, the brook sound is soft and gushing.

At 1.2 miles you reach a small clearing where several signs

Osmore Pond & Little Deer Mountain

are posted. A brown and white one points straight ahead for the Osmore Pond Hiking Loop.

After a short walk along the loop, you'll see the waters of Osmore Pond. The peaceful trail winds gently around the pond's edge. It parallels the eastern shoreline about fifty feet away. Two footpaths lead to clear views at the edge of this lovely, isolated pond. Rising above the southwestern end is Little Deer Mountain.

The sturdy log structures you pass are some of the more than twenty-five group camping lean-tos in the Groton State Forest. They may be used for wilderness camping according to the forest rules. In addition, state personnel maintain 225 individual camping sites.

You pass through occasional spruce bogs as the way continues around the pond. At the northern tip, the trail veers away from the water. You pick your way over a boggy area and small stream-let. As the path continues along the western shore, it closely follows the water's edge. Watch carefully for the blue-blazed trail markers. Short young spruces and heavy side growth struggle to hide the trail.

Big Deer Mountain rises above the eastern shore of Osmore Pond. Nearby, sun-bleached logs poke their bulk above the water's surface. If you quietly approach one of these logs on a warm sunny day you may see pond sliders or other turtles basking in the sun.

Nearing the southern end of the pond, the trail winds gradually to the right. Power lines appear overhead. The path swings sharply left to a multi-signed trail junction.

Signs point straight ahead to Lake Groton, Peacham Pond, and Big Deer Mountain. Turn right here and follow the path beneath the power lines. After approximately 100 yards you will come to a sign pointing the way to Little Deer Mountain. It is .4 miles to the summit from here. Go right onto the path.

The blue-blazed trail maintains a moderate pitch. After a short distance it makes a 90-degree turn to the left. Watch carefully for the blue blazes at this point. The trail remains smooth and very enjoyable as it continues its moderate climb.

Near the summit the path swings left and leads into a small cleared area. There are limited views of nearby hills and an open look down the length of Lake Groton. To the southwest is Spruce Mountain, its high, pointed peak topped by a tower.

Hike back down the same trail to the sign for Little Deer Mountain. Go left onto the path beneath the power line and back to the signed intersection. Go right toward Lake Groton, Big Deer Mountain, and Peacham Pond.

Once again orange reflectorized diamonds mark this as a multi-purpose trail. Because of its narrowness and roughness, it could only be recommended to hikers and snowshoers, however. Bearing left, the path crosses a log bridge. The brook beneath is the outlet of Osmore Pond. This is the start of the gurgling brook which parallels the initial trail.

A series of short stumps have been placed on the trail to aid your passage over a final boggy area. Shortly after crossing this wet section you return to the junction of the Osmore Hiking Loop, Big Deer Mountain Trail, and the trail to Lake Groton. You have now hiked 4 miles and have 1.2 miles left on the trail to Lake Groton back to your car.

Osmore Pond & Little Deer Mountain

35. Big Deer Mountain

Class: II
Elevation: 1,992 feet
Vertical rise: 912 feet
Distance (round trip): 4.6 miles
Hiking time: 3 hours

This hike offers you another nice way to spend your time in Groton State Forest (see Hike 34). Some entrances to trails are closed after Labor Day, but the one described here remains open.

Because the trail to Big Deer is both pretty and gentle all along its 2.3 mile length, it does not depend upon spectacular views for its charm. The flat, rolling path would be an ideal foliage walk in the fall. Maples, elms, and birches surround the occasional balsams and spruces. An openness along the sides of the trail inspires a sense of freedom, and offers deep views into the woods.

Turn in at the green and yellow "Groton State Forest" sign which lists Lake Groton, Stillwater, and Big Deer. Continue straight on this road (it starts out paved but turns to gravel) for 1.8 miles. A small unsigned footpath (the Cold Water Brook Trail) leads left into the woods here. There is limited parking along the right edge of the road shortly before the path. Just beyond, a brook passes beneath the road.

The Cold Water Brook Trail climbs a small embankment and

Cold Water Brook

Big Deer Mountain

winds gently through the forest. Gains in elevation are hardly noticeable because of the steady, gradual rise.

The path slithers around large rocks. It passes through clusters of sparkling white birches as the hillside begins to slope steeply down to the right. The waters of Cold Water Brook can intermittently be seen and heard below.

Rolling along over slight dips and rises, the trail veers left past a large triangular boulder. Several black, muddy patches are crossed before the flat path enters stands of spruces and balsams bunched closely along the way. Re-entering the hardwood forest, the slender trees appear again.

After approximately ¼ mile the trail appears to fork. Keep left here. Take time to observe the various kinds of greenery all around. Lady fern and spinulose woodfern swarm around hobblebush and striped maple. Close to ground level you can see shining club moss, bunchberries, and ground pine.

Winding peacefully through the woods, the trail passes two large glacial boulders guarding the sloping fields of fern to the left. The way narrows and becomes rootier as it swings right. The left hillside draws closer to the trail.

A gentle brook tumbles across the path at approximately .9 miles. Water caresses the many round mossy stones herded between its edges. Beyond the brook the trail swings sharply left before winding right toward Cold Water Brook.

The roar of gushing water draws your attention to the right. Stop here for a delightful, shady respite. The brook's flowing softness turns frenzied as it rushes through a wide rocky chute. White water and foam gush into a quieter pool below. An archway in the huge-stoned wall flanking the brook allows some water to flow to the edge, while most continues over a low dam into a placid pool beyond.

Continuing up the moderate incline, you approach a fork in the trail. The Cold Water Brook Trail continues left here. It passes through light woods before crossing a small brook. Paralleling this brook awhile, it crosses again and begins a moderate climb to the right.

Glacial boulders protrude from the open woods as the path becomes rockier. It leads over the rounded stones of an old stream bed before returning to its flat, packed-dirt ways.

At 1.9 miles you enter a clearing with many signs. Follow the Big Deer Mountain sign upward to the right. You pass through expansive stands of first white, then yellow birch, as the way steepens.

At 2.1 miles another sign turns the path sharply right. From here you are approximately .2 miles from the summit. Proceed up the moderate grade through slender birches. Climbing over and around boulders, the trail begins to steepen. Its edges are dotted by reindeer lichen. Their tiny antlered design makes them look like clumps of snowflakes on the ground.

The path leads onto a flat ledged area surrounded by slim trees. A large blue blaze on a short stump marks the end of the trail. You have a somewhat limited view through the trees to the northeast.

Your return will be by the same route.

Big Deer Mountain

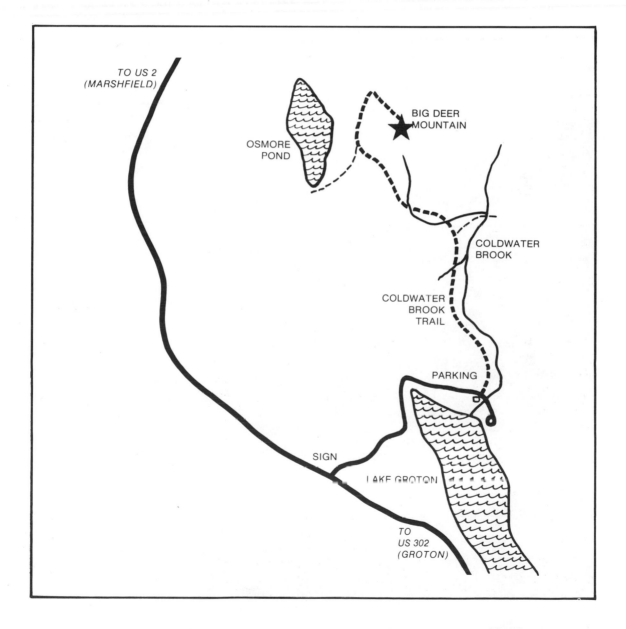

TO US 2
(MARSHFIELD)

OSMORE
POND

BIG DEER
MOUNTAIN

COLDWATER
BROOK

COLDWATER
BROOK
TRAIL

PARKING

SIGN

LAKE GROTON

TO
US 302
(GROTON)

Big Deer Mountain

Camel's Hump from Dean Trail

Camel's Hump

At 4,083 feet, Camel's Hump is Vermont's third highest mountain (tied with Mount Ellen) and rates as one of the finest hikes in the east. Try to climb this peak on a clear day. A mist-and-cloud enshrouded summit is a disappointing reward for the effort expended getting there.

Early French explorers gave the mountain its most appropriate name, the Couching Lion (*Le Lion Couchant*). From both east and west, its profile does resemble that of a resting lion. Victorians, who quivered at a subsequent title, "Camel's Rump," dubbed the mountain Camel's Hump.

There are a number of attractive paths to choose from in the Camel's Hump trail system, approachable from either North Duxbury or Huntington Center. You can mix and match them to form a hike tailored to your own taste. The combination of trails described here forms a solid day's hiking over primarily steep, rugged terrain.

To reach the start of the Callahan Trail on the mountain's east side, drive south on Vt. 100 from Waterbury. Follow it to the right where it splits from U.S. 2 and continue to the 90-degree left

36. Camel's Hump

Class: V
Elevation: 4,083 feet
Vertical rise: 2,640 feet
Distance (around loop): 6.9 miles
Hiking time: 6 hours

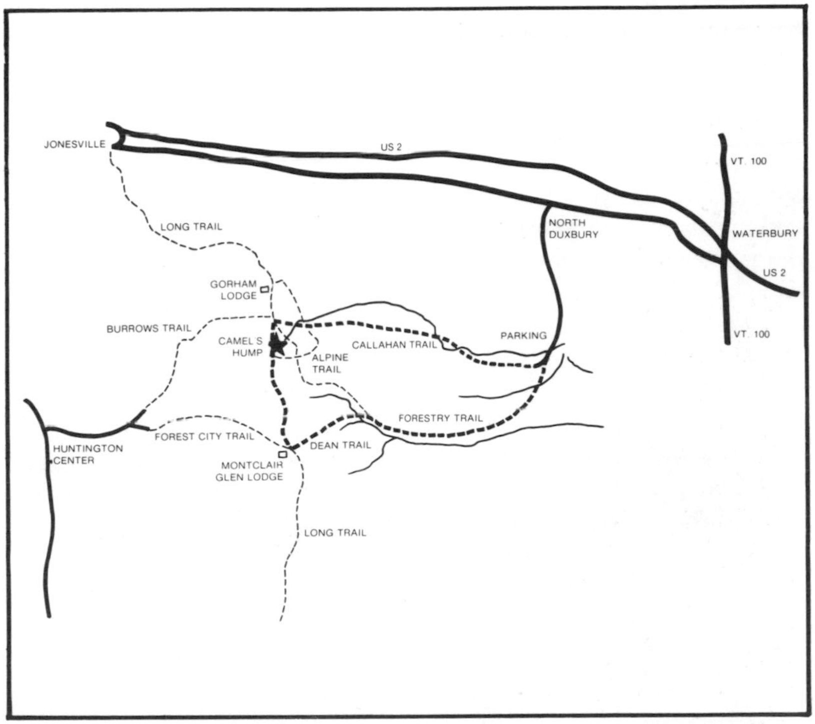

curve (a red school house is on the right here). Leave Vt. 100 and drive straight ahead onto the gravel road. Remain on this road for 5 miles. At that point, a buff-sided, black-roofed barn complex appears on the left. Turn south onto the gravel road just beyond the barns and follow it 3.5 miles to its end at the Monroe Parking Lot.

Camel's Hump State Park was established in 1969, in hopes of preserving at least one Green Mountain in a natural state. There is no camping allowed and no fires are permitted on the trails. Green Mountain Club lodges are available for overnight use. Fees are 50¢ for club members and 75¢ for non-members.

At the far end of the parking lot, a pipe bubbles fresh water into a rock-walled well. The water is cold and delicious. If you have fluoridated water in your canteen, change it here.

The Callahan Trail starts beside this watering spot and is marked by pale blue blazes. The trail begins wide and flat. It quickly crosses a narrow brook. A brown and white sign informs you that there are 2.2 miles to the junction of the Long Trail and 2.5 miles to the Camel's Hump summit.

Callahan Trail is well-maintained, as are all the trails on Camel's Hump. Long logs are positioned across the path, beside trenched areas, to prevent rain and melting snow runoff from eroding the trail. Shorter logs mold the embankment into stepped areas over some of the sharply inclined sections. The trail is unobstructed by twigs, brush, or litter.

Faster running water crosses the path at the .7 mile point. You'll find few flat resting areas along this trail, so stop here to refresh yourself before resuming the steady, steep climb to the summit.

A rat-a-tap-tap noise amongst the trees will announce the presence of yellow-bellied sapsuckers. These birds inhabit the open woods in summer months. Sapsuckers feast on the soft inner bark and sap of trees. The birds

Camel's Hump

sport black-and-white feathered backs and wings, red patches on their heads (and throats for males) and—sure enough—yellow bellies.

An interlude of white birches soothes your senses as the incline challenges your body. The trail crawls over and around rugged boulders. Giant rocks hang ominously above on the left, while the hillside drops off sharply below.

The Alpine Trail crosses the Callahan Trail at approximately 1.8 miles. Yellow blazes clearly mark this path. To the right a cold stream courses along. Follow the blue blazes of the Callahan Trail as they parallel the stream, then move upward and away.

At 2.2 miles the Callahan and Long trails meet in a grassy clearing. Turn left (south) and follow the Long Trail to the summit. White or white-and-orange blazes mark the way. Please walk only on the rocks, to protect the fragile vegetation of this area.

The Long Trail makes a winding, wind-buffeted ascent to the summit of Camel's Hump. Views extend north and south along the Green Mountains to Canada and Killington Peak, west to the Adirondacks and Lake Champlain, and east to the White Mountains.

The yellow-blazed Alpine Trail intersects with the Long Trail just below the summit. Continue south on the Long Trail. This descent is a steep one, but you will be rewarded intermittently by views north to the cone of Camel's Hump and east to an eye-stretching vista of mountains and valleys. The Long Trail here is persistently ledged and rockied. Patches of boggy black mud offer the only change.

As the Long Trail crosses the ridge and descends the east side, beaver ponds become visible below. More climbing and sliding down over rock and scrub bring you to the junction of the Dean Trail after 4½ miles of hiking.

Go left onto the blue-blazed Dean Trail. It is 1 mile from this point to its intersection with the Forestry Trail. The Dean Trail is mostly wet and muddy as it winds through the boggy area abutting the beaver ponds to the left. After approximately 5¼ miles (from the hike's start), you'll come upon Ridley Brook. The water courses quickly over and around its boulder-full bed.

At the intersection of the Dean Trail and the Forestry Trail (5.5 miles) you are approximately 1½ miles from the Monroe Parking Area. Turn right onto the blue-blazed Forestry Trail. This path makes a gradual descent over a broad, packed-dirt trail with occasional obstructing boulders and roots. Near its end the trail becomes a grassed-over road which intersects with a gravel one. Go left here. This road meets the main gravel road at right angles. A left turn and a short walk will bring you back to your car.

View of Camel's Hump from East

37. Mount Hunger

Class: IV
Elevation: 3,539 feet
Vertical rise: 2,259 feet
Distance (round trip): 3.8 miles
Hiking time: 4 hours

As the highest peak in the Worcester Range, 3,539-foot Mount Hunger commands superb views. Waterbury Valley and Reservoir nestle serenely to the west. Above and beyond, Green Mountain peaks extend south from Mount Mansfield. In all directions, mountains and valleys stretch before your eyes.

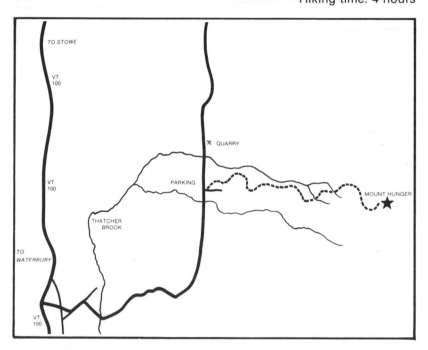

The Waterbury Center Trail is one of three routes to the summit; the other two begin in Shady Rill and Worcester. Turn off Vt. 100 at the sign for Waterbury Center Post Office. Follow this road to its end. Go left at the stop sign. Take the first right at the sign for Loomis Hill. Stay on this road for 3 miles and turn right onto a dirt road.

After approximately 200 feet, park in the tiny area on the left. Watch carefully for the two-foot high cairn on the left which marks the start of the trail. The path begins directly behind the cairn.

The path, unnamed and marked by white blazes, starts on an old grassy logging road, bounded by red pine. These stately trees have an optimistic uplift to their branch tips. You can recognize them by their long (three- to six-inch) needles in clusters of two. (Jack pine also has two-clustered needles, but they are three-quarters to one-and one-half-inches long.) The red pine's two- to three-inch cones grow directly on the twig.

Along the trail beyond the pines you'll find closed gentians. These tall plants have narrow leaves and usually grow in damp areas. Their bluish-purple flowers, which grow in clusters, appear in mid-to-late summer.

Climbing upward, the trail shifts from a logging road to a dirt- and rock-strewn path through open woods. You hear a wind-like sound to the left. The sound becomes louder as the trail swings upward to the right. Cresting a small knoll, you discover a rushing stream below.

At about the ¼-mile point the trail appears to stop in front of a towering boulder. Don't be misled by the opening to the right. Go left and follow the path up around the rock.

The trail swings sharply left around two tall red spruces

Mount Hunger

and assumes a moderate pitch. It will maintain this angle all the way to the ledges near the summit. The way is still soft underfoot and free of rocks and roots. Striped maples continue to line the path.

The way leads upward through a typical hardwood forest of maple, beech, elm, and hemlock. It swings right and follows an old stream bed cluttered with logs and stones. The logs disappear, but the trail continues along the gully, sometimes in it and sometimes alongside it.

Walking through this area, you notice the yellow birches. Both sides of the trail are crowded with these buff- and silver-colored trees. Further along, as if to remind you that they are not to be forgotten, large, smooth-faced white birches dot the way.

At the 1-mile point the trail leads up over several long sections of ledge. Water trickles down the path, making it wet and slippery. Red blazes cross the trail, marking the state-park boundary line.

The way has become increasingly rock-filled and demands careful stepping. The trail swings right, under and around a knoll, and

rises steeply through a maze of white birches. The birch pattern has now been reversed: whites predominate, and yellows have been left behind.

Balsam firs begin to appear as the path weaves over a network of roots and crosses a trickling stream at 1¼ miles. Trees are shorter, indicating that you are reaching higher elevations. The path bears left and flattens out for a short distance, providing a respite for wearied legs.

A second, slowly moving stream crosses the path at the 1½-mile mark. Pause here for a cooling drink or a soothing footbath in the clear, cold water.

The dwarfed trees of the higher elevations offer less protection.

Temperatures drop and winds blow increasingly stronger. Perpendicular ledge makes the climbing more difficult. Hands and walking sticks must aid your feet here. Hiking becomes a slow, step-at-a-time process.

Note well the direction of the trail as it approaches the summit. The white blazes blend perfectly with patches of white quartz in the ledge, making it hard to recognize the trail at times. An extra check on the way up may save uncertain moments on the return trip.

A bare limb supported by many stones marks the summit. The surrounding area is barren, except for several dwarfed spruce no more than three feet high. Wind scours the area.

Mount Hunger

38. Elmore Mountain

Class: III
Elevation: 2,608 feet
Vertical rise: 1,528 feet
Distance (round trip): 3 miles
Hiking time: 2¼ hours

A day or two of varied outdoor recreation awaits you at Elmore State Park. Situated around the shores of Lake Elmore, the park includes a half-mile beach and a hiking trail to the summit of Elmore Mountain. Before or after hiking you'll have opportunities to camp or picnic; go swimming, boating or fishing; and—if you didn't bring your own food—visit the refreshment stand.

Enter the park from Vt. 12, 4.3 miles southeast of Morrisville. To reach the hiking trail, proceed straight from the entrance booth toward the picnic area. The road swings left and begins to curve right, when a sharp right turn suddenly appears. Take this turn, and follow it to a thick wire crossing the road. Park on the right, just before the wire.

The trail to Elmore Mountain begins as a gravel road and winds gradually upward. Varied trees and flowers line the way.

The trail becomes slightly steeper. Red blazes on trees to the left appear at the half-mile mark. Don't mistake them for trail markers; they indicate the state-park boundary.

View from summit of Elmore Mountain to Mount Hunger and Worcester Range

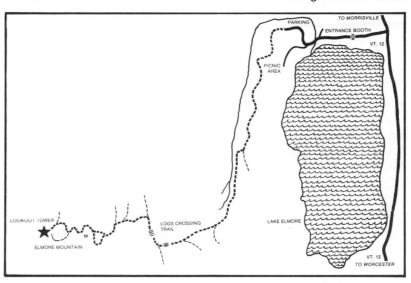

A few steps farther along you will see a sign for Elmore Tower on a yellow birch at the right side of the trail. It requests that you "carry out what you carry in." A red metal arrow points the way.

Turn right here and walk up the split log steps. Pass between large beech trees with bark scarred by carved initials and names. The trail is wide and comfortable underfoot as it swings to parallel a small brook on the right. A short side path leads down to the water, which flows freely and tastes good.

As the way leads upward to the right, occasional log-braced trenches appear. Crossing the path, they divert runoff water before it can build up and damage the trail.

At .8 miles the smooth, flat trail splits. While it looks as if the bigger path goes straight, another red arrow points right. Follow its direction onto a steeper, rockier path.

Just before reaching a group of large boulders, note that another trail joins the one you are on, from the left. On your return, remember to stay left at this unmarked fork.

The trail winds right, and then

Elmore Mountain

up to the left. It crosses two areas where logs have been placed atop wet spots. Beyond these logs another path intersects from the left. Just beyond this intersection, logs again provide firm footing across the wet trail. Remember that, after crossing this last set of logs on the way back, the left trail is the one to take.

A red arrow points to a 90-degree turn to the left. The trail is still a pleasant dirt path, relatively free of stones and roots. Telephone lines pass almost directly overhead as it joins another path, entering from the right. The two continue upward as one. Note the two large maple trees (one functioning as a telephone pole) at this junction, and turn right here on your return trip.

The trail steepens as it gains altitude. It goes through a wet, muddy area and approaches a high, steep ledge. If you are ambitious, climb straight up. A more gradual way swings left and meets this shortcut atop the ledge.

Climbing quite steeply, you will top a crest at the 1¼-mile mark and step into a surprisingly picturesque setting. Four beautiful white birches form a rectangular

perimeter around a picnic table straight ahead. Behind and to the left of the grassy clearing a small cabin with stone chimney sits on a knoll overlooking Lake Elmore. The ranger and his family live here six months of the year.

A fine view to the east across Lake Elmore opens from an overlook at the left edge of the clearing. If you are not anxious to climb the very steep and narrow ¼-mile trail to the summit, this view provides an acceptable substitute.

The trail follows white painted arrows up the ledge to the summit. Although the climb is demand-

ing, the reward at the top will make the effort worthwhile.

Climb the lookout tower for a beautiful view. With the exception of the Worcester Range immediately to the south, Elmore Mountain is the highest point in the area. You gaze out over endless miles of rolling hills and manicured farms separated by patches of dark green trees.

The black and white forms of cows dot the open fields and the sun reflects off silos and metal roofs. The impression is one of awesome vastness; the mood, peaceful and relaxed as you look to the horizons.

Elmore Mountain

39. Blake Pond

Class: II
Elevation: 1,660 feet
Vertical rise: 580 feet
Distance (round trip): 5.8 miles
Hiking time: 3 hours

Elmore Mountain and Lake Elmore

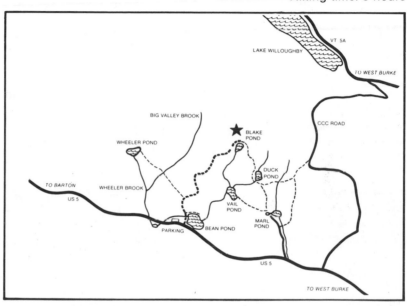

Blake Pond is one of many primitive ponds cradled within Willoughby State Forest's 6,700 acres. The trail to it, like others in the forest, provides a nice chance to quietly enjoy nature and, at the same time, limber up your muscles for more strenuous hikes. You can spend hours just wandering through the beautiful scenery of this area.

Blake Pond Trail offers an excellent introduction to this attractive trail system. Drive to the Willoughby State Forest parking area off U.S. 5. It is located 5.5 miles south of the junction of route 5 and Vt. 16 in Barton and 7.2 miles north of the junction of route 5 and Vt. 5A in West Burke. Walk south from the parking lot and turn left onto the dirt road.

Follow this road to the sturdy, slatted, wooden bridge crossing the outlet of Bean Pond. Look southeast across the pond for a good view of Norris Mountain.

Continue along the dirt road and take the left fork when it divides shortly beyond the bridge. This narrow rocky road makes

its way up a small grade. At the top it forks, and a brown board sign etched with white letters guides you to the right toward Blake Pond.

Beeches, sugar maples, and white birches parade beside the trail. The way is intermittently dark and light as trees touch branches overhead, blocking much of the sky light. Then they are interrupted by groups of waist-high goldenrod and wood asters. Butterflies and bees dart and swoop between the blossoms.

Much of the way is steep. The trail turns sharply to the right

and continues its bending uphill route. Watch for the tiny toads that scuttle about your feet (they seem to get underfoot before you notice them).

At .9 miles tall grass and spreading shrubs start to overrun the path as it levels off, giving your muscles a well-earned rest. After ¼ mile more, however, you'll climb the steepest grade of this rutted, rocky road. Ferns grow luxuriantly along the trail. Although there are no trail markers, the roadway is so obvious that you won't get lost.

A number of young and mature

Blake Pond

striped maples fill this area. These slender trees can be readily identified by their large, three-lobed leaves and smooth black-and-white streaked bark.

After 1.7 miles the trail winds to the left and widens. Open woodland areas appear along the way as it rises and falls. Walking becomes much less arduous.

More brown and white board signs direct you at 2.8 miles. On the right, one points straight ahead to Duck Pond. To the left, another aims back down the trail to Bean Pond.

Shortly after these signs the road forks. A sign between the two arms of the fork indicates that you have arrived at Blake Pond. The water is visible through the trees to the right. If you approach quietly, you may surprise a wading blue heron or feeding ducks.

Return to your car by the same route.

View of Blake Pond

Blake Pond

40. Wheeler Mountain

Class: III
Elevation: 2,371 feet
Vertical rise: 711 feet
Distance (around loop): 3.1 miles
Hiking time: 2½ hours

Wheeler Mountain's pleasant, well-marked hiking trails abound with a refreshing variety of topographical features and some of the best views from any of the mountains in this area. Climb on a clear, sunny day.

From Little Peak, one of the elevated vantage points near the summit, you look to the northwest and Jay Peak. Eagle Cliff, a second overlook, offers a view which unfolds across smooth manicured farmlands and Lake Willoughby to Bald Mountain. Mount Pisgah towers above the southeastern tip of the lake.

The dirt road to the Wheeler Mountain trails runs north from U.S. 5, 8.1 miles north of the intersection of route 5 and Vt. 5A in West Burke, and 4.6 miles south of the intersection of route 5 and Vt. 16 in Barton. It weaves past Wheeler Pond and, after 2 miles, stops at the second of two farmhouses on the right. Park in the open area on the left. The trail begins here.

The path crosses the open field. Trembling aspen appear on the right. Common throughout Vermont, these yellow-green trees flourish in dry woods and old fields. The leaves are rounded, come to a sharp point, and have

Wheeler Mountain

small even teeth. The leaf stalks are slim and flat, causing the leaves to "tremble" easily in the wind.

The path across the open field leads gradually upward. After walking for .2 miles, you reach a sign on two steel supports. The trail divides here. A steep, 1.35-mile trail, marked by red blazes, goes right. A more gradual 1.85-mile, white-blazed trail leads to the left. The former trail will be your return route.

The white-blazed trail continues across the open field. Blueberry bushes abound, and reward you

with a summer treat. Flowers, shrubs, and grass crowd the path as it approaches the woods.

As you proceed through stands of tall maples and birches, spinulose woodfern gather along the left side of the way. The trail winds to the right, then quickly left, and crosses Wheeler Brook. You leave the overgrown field behind.

Continuing steadily upward, the way passes a large boulder, gripped octopus-like by an old stump's entwining roots. Here the trail curves sharply right, then proceeds upward to the left.

Wheeler Mountain

Just beyond the ½-mile mark, the way becomes very steep. Woodfern smother the areas on both sides of the path. Roots and large rocks cover the trail as you pass a huge, beautiful, white birch, clinging resolutely to the path's edge.

The path weaves beneath towering balsams which blanket the hillside. Roots from these trees interlock across the trail, making it rough and spongy. Step carefully here to avoid slipping.

Still winding steeply upward through towering firs, the trail swings between large moss- and lichen-textured boulders at .6 miles. It is snaked with roots and softened by fir spills.

The trail dips abruptly down into a small gully and then heads upward across an open ledge. Look to your right. The view includes Wheeler Pond, with Norris and companion mountains in the background.

Another vista appears shortly on the right (south). The path proceeds through a small stand of red spruce and suddenly leads onto a large area of bare ledge. Here, at the .9-mile mark, the white- and the red-blazed trails meet and continue as one toward the summit.

A few feet farther along you will see a sign indicating the route to Little Peak. Climb the 100-foot spur for a prime view to the northwest. Return to the combined trail. The trails separate briefly and rejoin again for the climb to the top.

The path crosses over and through alternating sections of ledge and alpine forest. It climbs up over a whale-shaped boulder, as peeling white birches scatter along the trail sides. An open area at 1.3 miles offers expansive views to the south.

The trail edges along the southern rim of Wheeler Mountain and then begins a steep ascent over ledge. After 1½ miles, you can look northwest toward Jay Peak and southwest toward Mount Mansfield.

The path descends sharply into a small ravine. It becomes narrow and squeezes between spruce and fir. A small register box to the right of the trail leads the way onto Eagle Cliff.

Retrace your steps from the cliff for ½ mile to where the white-blazed trail goes right and the red-blazed trail leads left. Go left down the steeper incline. Follow this path until it rejoins the white-blazed trail, after

100 yards. The combined trails will return you to the open ledge where the two divide once again.

Descend via the red-blazed trail over bare ledges crusted with black lichen. The way is steep and straight, with frequent switchbacks. Approximately one mile from the summit at Eagle Cliff, the path winds through a forested area and leaves the ledges above.

Small gnarled roots grip the trail as it dips down into cool, mapled woods. Your feet leave rock, and return to the packed-dirt trail. The path bursts into the field after 1.2 miles and rejoins the white-blazed trail. Travel back across the field to your car.

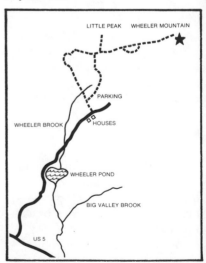

Wheeler Mountain

41. Mount Pisgah

Class: III
Elevation: 2,751 feet
Vertical rise: 1,491 feet
Distance (around loop): 6.9 miles
Hiking time: 4½ hours

Sheer-faced Mount Pisgah forms the towering southeastern perimeter of Lake Willoughby. Its trails are noted for their prime views of the lake, the northern Green Mountains and the Burke Mountain-Victory Bog Wilderness.

The South Trail to Mount Pisgah begins on Vt. 5A, 5.6 miles south of the junction of routes 5A and 16 in Westmore. You'll see the brown and white South Trail sign at the eastern side of the highway approximately ½ mile south of Lake Willoughby. Leave your car in the area directly across the road.

The trail follows a grown-over road through a small meadow. After a couple of hundred yards, yellow blazes appear to the left. Watch closely for this trail marker: a yellow blaze on a white birch tree. From here on the trail is regularly and clearly marked.

A wide, relatively smooth path winds its way through blazing white birches and begins a climb through open woods. Boulders form islands in the trail. The path is alternately easy, then rugged going as it passes moss-covered rocks. If you'll believe a favorite uncle's tale about

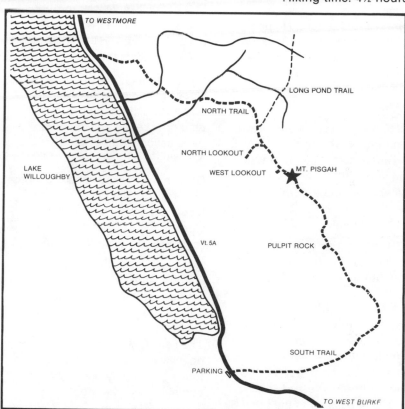

Indian blood causing the rocks to turn green, this area must have been a major battleground.

The trail swings 90 degrees to the left at a brown and white sign after ¼ mile. The steep grade persists as you pick your way over the rockied path. The way widens and smooths out, but continues its upward climb.

After ½ mile the path switches back right, then left, and proceeds up a rocky embankment. Near the top, a 40-foot spur leads off to the left. It takes you to the first of the open views from the South Trail. A second area offers open western views 300 feet farther along the main trail.

Mount Pisgah

Leaving this latter vista, walk upward to the right. Numbers of lovely white birch flank the trail on both sides. They sparkle among the surrounding greens and greys of the forest.

At .8 miles a yellow and brown sign guides you to Pulpit Rock, elevation 1,710 feet. Due west are views of Mount Hor and Wheeler Mountain, while the southern end of Lake Willoughby lies directly below.

The largest fish ever caught in Vermont came from Lake Willoughby's deep waters. On May 8, 1960, Leon E. Hopkins landed a forty-six-inch lake trout that weighed thirty-four pounds and had a twenty-five-inch girth. The fish was so heavy that Leon had to beach it to get it out of the water. This record specimen can be seen at the Leon E. Hopkins & Son Insurance Agency on Church Street in Lyndonville, Vermont.

The rest of the climb to the summit is unrelentingly steep. It passes over and around boulders and makes a sharp swing left around a massive elm. White birches give way to beeches and maples.

The path picks its way through stone-strewn areas. At 1¼ miles a medium-sized, yellow-blazed boulder bisects the path.

Balsam fir begin to populate the slopes as the grey, broad-leaf forest melds into the green alpine one. Ledge appears and trees become abbreviated in height.

Grey, mica-flecked sand crunches underfoot as the climb over bare ledge steepens. Natural depressions in the rock, and clinging roots provide good footholds.

At 1.6 miles you'll be encouraged by a group of signs indicating that the true summit is only 500 feet away. A brown and yellow sign marks this point. The heavily wooded summit has no views. A nearby mailbox, looking strangely out of place, contains a register book.

Leave the summit via the North Trail (also yellow-blazed). About ¼ mile from the summit you will reach the spur to Lookout #1 (West Lookout). Wind your way to the left for a vertical view of Lake Willoughby and awesome views of surrounding peaks. Mount Hor is the closest peak to the west. Wheeler Mountain is the rock-faced peak to the north-

west. The total view extends sixty miles from Lake Memphremagog and Jay Peak to Camel's Hump and beyond.

Rejoin the North Trail and continue a short distance to the spur for Lookout #2 (North Lookout). Turn left. White signs with black arrows guide you along this narrow, curving trail.

Re-trace your steps to the North Trail and turn left onto it. This cool, shaded path descends gradually. Low bushes threaten to choke portions of it at times. The way becomes steeper and leads over black, spongy earth past several massive moss-covered stumps.

The path takes a sharp bend to the right and drops steeply left. At a fork, the Long Pond Trail goes right. Stay on the North Trail to the left. The path descends steeply and rapidly. This is prime ankle-spraining territory. Pick you way carefully.

At a less extreme angle, the trail courses along a small gully over an old stream bed. At 3.5 miles you must rock hop across a clear-running stream.

The trail parallels this stream and turns right as the gurgling quiets in the background. A sec-

Mount Pisgah

und stream crosses the path shortly thereafter.

The North Trail continues over gentle hills and gullies. It turns sharply left and begins the steeper descent to route 5A.

Once at the road you have a pleasant 2.7-mile walk along Lake Willoughby to your car.

View across Lake Willoughby to Mount Pisgah

Mount Pisgah

Monarch Butterfly

We told you earlier (see Hike 12) that there are a lot of Bald Mountains in Vermont. Here's another one. The hike to this Bald Mountain—in Westmore—is both challenging and pretty. Wild flowers, beautiful in summer, snuggle close along the way. The perky brightness of yellow king devil, purple and white wood asters, and goldenrod gaily introduce you to the Bald Mountain Trail.

To reach the start of the trail turn off Vt. 5A at the white Westmore Congregational Church, 1 mile south of the junction of Vt. 16 and 5A, and 4 miles north of the southern end of Lake Willoughby. Follow this paved road for .6 miles to the fork. Go right on the paved road (it soon turns to gravel). After 1.3 miles the road forks again. Bear right here (a large glacial boulder can be seen in the field to the left) and continue on this gravel road for 1.8 miles. Watch for a narrow dirt road on the right marked by a weathered sign saying: "Hall Mountain Fire Tower." It is best to park here just off the main road.

The rutted, mirey back road to the beginning of the trail is not always passable for cars and can be navigated most easily on foot. Follow this road .6 miles to a grassy fork. Go left, and follow the path over the wooden bridge spanning Bald Mountain Brook. The water here is clear and cold. The trail is unmarked but easy to follow, as it is the only one to the summit from this side.

Immediately after you cross the bridge, the way is straight and heavily wooded. A walk of 150 yards brings you to a large clearing on the left. Near its far end a wooden marker points to an unmarked trail cutting sharply right. Take this.

The path proceeds in a straight line through a thin forest of young trees. Parallel and to the left, a small brook tumbles through the shady coolness of the woods. Sunlight filters down through the trees, freckling the trail with light and shadow.

Telephone wires cross the path at the 1-mile mark and will continue to, all the way to the summit. The way narrows and becomes more rocky. Water makes it slippery in spots.

Bald Mountain

42. Bald Mountain (Westmore)

Class: III
Elevation: 3,315 feet
Vertical rise: 1,595 feet
Distance (round trip): 5.8 miles
Hiking time: 4½ hours

If you haven't already done so, watch for scurrying wildlife. The trail teems with assorted toe-level creatures. Toads abound; field mice and salamanders are also plentiful. Trail lore has it that toads seen in abundance foretell rain. Their species vary greatly in both size and color, but almost all will remain motionless for your further inspection after their initial, frightened leap.

The path remains straight and gradual. Maples and birches stand like slender, sinewy youngsters chaperoned by occasional mature pines. A bit further along, bunchberry and hemlock begin to appear.

At approximately 1.4 miles the trail narrows and becomes little more than a footpath through the woods. Grass, weeds, and flowers entangle in the path as it winds upward. The dirt trail becomes barely wide enough for your feet.

Slender barkless logs form steps across the muddy way at 1¾ miles. The black mud continues for 200 yards as more steps hold the trail together.

At approximately 2 miles the trail levels out temporarily be-

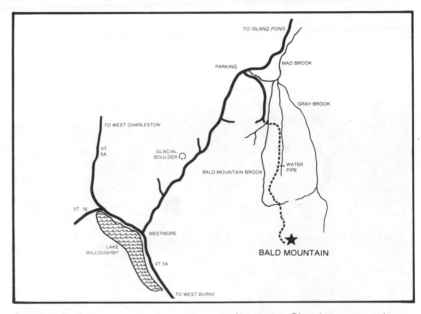

fore beginning an upward surge. At this point your legs and lungs will probably let you know you've reached the steepest part of the trail so far.

A pipe extends from the small brook to the left edge of the way at 2.2 miles. Although it's not a reliable source, you may stop here in the spring for a refreshing drink before tackling the rise to the summit.

At 2.5 miles the trail makes its first sharp turn diagonally up to the left, passing between scattered white birches. It then swings sharply right and becomes

quite steep. Slender roots grip the path like fingers while majestic white birches, sandwiched between green hemlocks, light the way.

The trail becomes wetter here. Pick your way carefully over the water-slicked stones and moss. Ledge intertwined with roots provides firm footing to the top. Mica and quartz sparkle along the way.

Approaching the summit you see first a brown shed, next, the Bald Mountain fire tower rising behind it. Climb the tower for a panoramic view in all directions.

Bald Mountain

Sparkling lakes nestle among rolling peaks as you scan the northeastern Vermont, southern Quebec, and northern New Hampshire countryside. A map in the tower answers your questions as you gaze out and down. Particularly striking are Bald Hill Pond and Newark Pond to the south.

If you have allowed ample time and still feel fresh, you might want to descend the 1.9 mile trail leading to Long Pond before returning to your car via the same trail you ascended.

Bald Mountain

13. Devil's Gulch

Class: II
Elevation: 1,300 feet
Vertical rise: 780 feet
Distance (round trip): 5 miles
Hiking time: 3 hours

This rough gouge in the earth abounds with ferns and moss-covered rocks. It is regarded by the Green Mountain Club as one of the most beautiful, secluded spots on the Long Trail. Its forbidding name adds a primitive lure all its own.

The access road to the portion of the Long Trail leading to Devil's Gulch is Vt. 118, the Eden-Belvidere Highway. Drive west from Eden 4.8 miles, or east from Belvidere Center 6.1 miles. Watch carefully for the white-painted "LT" and arrow on the rocky ledge to the north side of the highway. There is limited parking in a grassy off-road area just east of this marker (Hike 44, to Belvidere Mountain begins at this point.)

Cross to the road's south side and follow the white blazes of the Long Trail up the embankment and into the woods. The path winds gently through young, lean trees.

After going beneath a power line, the way emerges into an overgrown pasture. Logs and boards have been laid on the path to help you over the wetter portions.

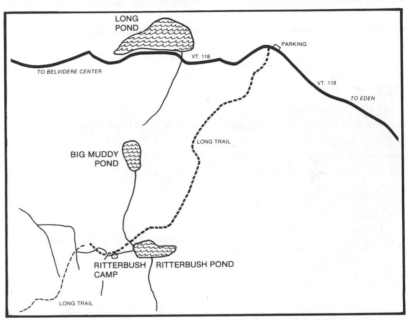

Deep within Devil's Gulch

Trailsides are thick with grasses and field flowers. You may see orange hawkweed or yellow king devil, yellow goldenrod or porcelain-blue closed gentian. Smooth-barked white pines spill needles across the trail. Green and white leaves of the trembling aspen shimmer as they are blown by wind and lit by sun.

Leaving the pasture, the trail enters open woods. Its upward course is still gentle. Few roots or stones roughen the way.

A variety of greenery begins to edge the path. One of the most striking specimens is striped maple, with its smooth, greenish bark vividly striped by black and white. In May its clusters of yellow flowers appear. The leaves are large, generally with three main lobes.

The trail twists easily up, over, and down gentle knolls. At a small clearing marked by patches of wet, black mud and large fallen trees, watch carefully for the white blazes as the path winds left. Shrubbery chokes the trail and thorned blackberry bushes tug at your legs.

Devil's Gulch

You must thrust your way through this thick growth and over wet areas.

A steep downslope may require some careful side-stepping. Generally, you lose elevation on your trek to Devil's Gulch. It's the exact opposite of climbing a mountain: the return trip (via the same route) will be the more trying one.

At 1½ miles a white and red sign marks a new section of the Long Trail. Follow its twisting way around and over logs. Unusual kinds of fungi scallop the trees and rotting logs.

Soon the path crosses a fast running stream. This is one of three dependable water sources on the trail. At the 2-mile point this new route rejoins the original Long Trail. Again, white and red signs clearly mark the way.

Another fast-flowing brook is crossed shortly. After winding steeply upward the trail approaches Ritterbush Camp. This small frame building was constructed in 1933 and can accommodate eight. (A toilet is provided—up a short trail to the left.) Walk to the back

right corner of the cabin and continue hiking.

The way leads steadily upward to a 90-degree turn where a white sign points left. Here, you may step out onto a small overlook to the right. Below, a stream courses through the middle of a tree- and shrub-choked gully.

Wind down to the right over a log footbridge into this gully. A miniature waterfall appears to the left. Hold your cupped hands beneath its flow and enjoy a refreshing drink.

Just ahead is a brief but rugged climb over moss-covered boulders and gnarled roots. The path levels again as stepping

stones offer footing across a dank-smelling, wet area. Ahead, massive hunks of rock form an A-shaped tunnel. After passing between them, you reach Devil's Gulch.

A jumble of boulders makes hiking a challenge. Above, ledge rises straight and steep on both sides. Ferns feather the surfaces of many of these gargantuan boulders. Cave-like depressions lurk among the rocks forming the gulch walls.

Stand still and survey these surroundings. The feeling is a primeval one—time seems to have stood still.

Return via the same route.

Devil's Gulch

44. Belvidere Mountain

Class: III
Elevation: 3,360 feet
Vertical rise: 2,080 feet
Distance (round trip): 5.6 miles
Hiking time: 4 hours

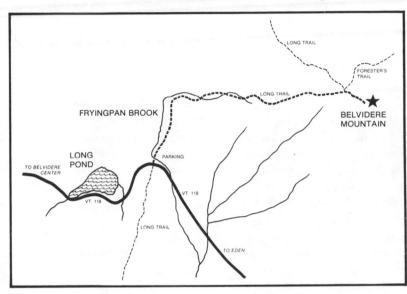

Belvidere Mountain is better known for its asbestos mines than for the expansive views available from its summit. Since 1936, when the Ruberoid Company began systematically mining its slopes, Belvidere has been a leader in producing asbestos. In the mid-1950s this one mountain yielded ninety-six percent of all the asbestos mined in the United States. An active mine at the eastern base of the mountain still supplies asbestos for shingles, cement, theater curtains, firemen's suits, brake linings, pipe coverings, and other products.

This hike begins opposite the one to Devil's Gulch. (See Hike 43.) The Long Trail crosses Vt. 118 at the high point of land located 4.8 miles west of Eden and 6.1 miles east of Belvidere Center on the Eden-Belvidere Highway. Look carefully along the ledge on the north side of the highway for the white-painted "LT" and arrow pointing upward. There is limited parking, just east of the marker.

To the right of the white arrow, the Long Trail leads up a small embankment. It parallels Frying

View of Belvidere Mountain showing asbestos mine

Pan Brook and then continues over old Vt. 118, crossing the fast-flowing brook in the process.

As the way leads into the woods it passes over several wet, boggy areas. Long logs aid the footing through this thickly muddied section. The path swings upward to the right around a yellow birch and continues to a large maple, which splits the trail. A former logging road leads right and the Long Trail goes left. Keep on the Long Trail.

The way steepens moderately, as the gully through which Frying Pan Brook runs appears below to the left. The trail keeps com-

pany with the brook for quite a distance, alternately paralleling and swinging away from it.

After ¼ mile an old logging road crosses the trail diagonally, and dips down to the brook. The brook's waters slither and slide over long stretches of flat rock.

The path intersects another logging road and continues along it to the left. The way suddenly becomes wider and flat.

A small trickle of water muddies the trail just before it takes a sharp swing to the right. It leads into a small, low, wet area and seems to stop. Although

Belvidere Mountain

not well-marked, the trail goes right here and climbs up over root-formed steps.

As the grade flattens out, the way becomes bumpy with rocks while it parallels the brook on the left. It criss-crosses and rises steeply alongside this miniature wilderness river. The water cascades through slender gouges, over rocks, and into shallow pools before gushing downward again.

More wet patches. The path crests a moderate slope and passes over two grassy roads in quick succession. Trail sides overflow with fern, hobblebush, and wood sorrel.

The way becomes very steep as it leads over roots and rocks. Trees thin out drastically at the top of the incline. A startlingly large patch of sky suddenly appears above. You are now approximately halfway to the top of Belvidere Mountain.

Leveling out a bit, the trail crosses an overgrown logging road. Trees become shorter as the way winds upward. It dips down into a small, very wet gully and finds firmer footing on old logs. You cross still another old road, as the trail passes through an open area and weaves left.

Narrowing to a mere footpath, the trail swings steeply right and passes over a long slab of ledge. It tunnels through thick stands of evergreens and is bathed in their fragrance. The path picks its way slowly over and around slippery, moss-covered rocks and roots.

Remaining narrow and steep, the trail continues upward to the four-way intersection at Belvidere Saddle between the two peaks of Belvidere Mountain. The unmarked Forester's Trail leads right, and extends .2 miles to the main summit. The way is very straight and moderately steep.

A lookout platform and a watchman's hut greet you at the summit. Climb the tower and enjoy the unfolding views.

To the east are the peaks around Lake Willoughby: Bald Mountain, Mount Pisgah, and Mount Hor, with the White Mountains of New Hampshire extending to the horizon. Swinging south, the Green Mountains are visible; Mansfield and Camel's Hump, particularly so. The Cold Hollow Mountains sit to the west, while Jay Peak and Big Jay rise prominently in the north. To the right of these twin peaks are Owl's Head and other Canadian peaks in the vicinity of Lake Memphremagog.

Return to your car by the same route.

Belvidere Mountain

45. Jay Peak

Class: IV
Elevation: 3,861 feet
Vertical rise: 1,661 feet
Distance (round trip): 3.4 miles
Hiking time: 3 hours

If you are striving to become a south-to-north end-to-ender on the Long Trail, Jay Peak's summit leaves you only ten miles short of your goal. A primitive wilderness until snow falls, Jay then transforms itself into a bustling center of winter activity and becomes one of the most popular ski areas in northern Vermont. Avid skiers think nothing of traveling hundreds of miles to ride its aerial tramway and make as many runs as time and money allow.

The Long Trail (your route to Jay's summit) crosses the Jay-Montgomery Center Road (Vt. 242) at the top of a long, steep grade between the two towns. The hike to Jay Peak begins on the north side of the highway, 5.1 miles west of Jay Village and 6.7 miles east of Montgomery Center. The Jay Peak Ski area road lies 1.3 miles to the east.

The Long Trail, marked by white blazes, begins across the road. The Atlas Valley Shelter sits on a knoll just above road level. The Atlas Plywood Division, over whose land the trail passes

Pleurotus Mushrooms

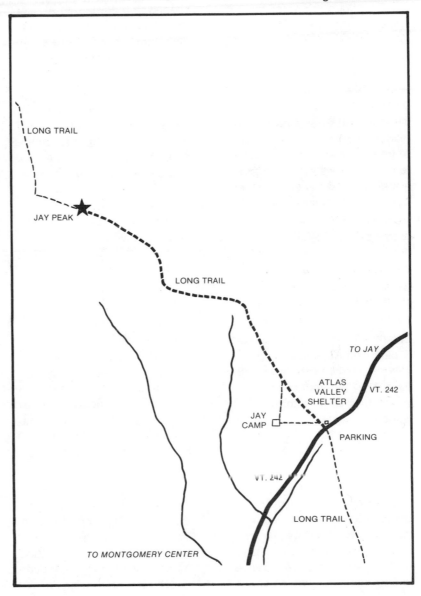

Jay Peak

here, provided this small ply-wood lean-to. Green Mountain Club members erected it in 1967. It is designed for day use by picnickers and hikers, but can accommodate three or four people overnight.

The trail begins as a narrow path leading upward through stands of young white birches. After a few minutes' walk, you approach a brown and white sign with accompanying register book. The Long Trail continues straight ahead while a side trail leads left to Jay Camp, .2 miles distant.

The way leads upward over an old stream bed. Rock faces are crinkled with moss and tiny pools of water dampen the way.

Beautiful yellow birches suddenly catch your eye as they parade down the hillside and across the path. They glimmer silvery yellow from deep within the woods.

As the trail from Jay Camp enters on the left, yellow birches begin to mix with the white birches to which they eventually give way. Hobblebush lines the path. Deer like to feed on the twigs and buds of this three-to eight-foot high shrub. Large white clusters of flowers appear in May and June, while pearl-shaped fruit develop in August and change from red to black at maturity. The leaves also change to a deep magenta color in the fall.

The path leads upward to the left, then dips quickly. Ferns, moss, hobblebush, and striped maple combine to produce heavy green sidegrowth along the way. Slightly higher up, common wood sorrel appears near ground level. It has three compound leaves and at a quick glance might be mistaken for clover. Its leaves taste tangy and refreshing.

Edging along the hillside, the path becomes more gradual. It continues like this for a fair distance, allowing legs and lungs to relax a bit.

Winding up through spruce and balsam, the way becomes rockier and steeper. Bunches of shining club moss cluster around tree bottoms. They look like small gardens of cactus nestled between the trees.

After approximately a mile the way leads out onto a large ski trail cut through the timberland. The 100-foot swath looks like the aftermath of a glacier that flattened everything in its path. Watch closely for white arrows and blazes here as the trail leads diagonally up to the left. It crosses the slope, and enters the woods to the right.

From here to just below the summit, the path crosses the ski slope several times. It rises sharply over ledge and small boulders cleared to the sides of the ski trail. Damp spots make the going slippery at times. The Christmas-tree smell of balsam fills the air and accompanies you upward.

The trail snakes through low scrub growth of spruce and balsam. You pass the small, metal-roofed hut of the ski patrol on the right and begin the final climb to the summit over bumpy ledge and two-foot-high alpine forests.

Cresting the final ledge, you'll find a high-powered telescope. It is available for public use if you have the necessary dime to fit the slot. With or without its aid the view is breathtaking, looking out to all directions and taking in rolling hills, towering peaks, flat farmland, winding roads, and long lakes.

Eastward, the view includes Lake Memphremagog; to the west, the Champlain Valley. The Green Mountains can be seen

Jay Peak

stretching southward as far as Lincoln Peak, while Owl's Head and other Canadian mountains rise to the north.

Your return is via the same trail, although you may want to try the open ski trail as a partial alternative descent route. It will bring you back to its original junction with the Long Trail. Go right here and follow the Long Trail back to your car.

Spider web

Jay Peak

Sunset Ridge Trail (Mount Mansfield)

Backpacking Hikes

Stratton Mountain

Your itinerary for this back-packing trip includes the 3,136-foot south peak of Stratton Mountain, trailside views of beaver ponds, and a night on the shores of Stratton Pond, the largest—and one of the most attractive—bodies of water on the Long Trail.

(Stratton Mountain's north peak, which houses the upper station of the Stratton Mountain Chair Lift, is bypassed. Should you want to visit this area, follow the .8-mile spur trail leading north from the fire tower on the south peak.)

First Day

Arlington-West Wardsboro Road to Stratton Mountain south peak, pond, and Stratton View Shelter

Class: III
Vertical rise: 1,616 feet
Distance: 6.2 miles
Hiking time: 3½ hours

The Stratton Mountain Trail starts on the Arlington-West Wardsboro Road. Driving east from Arlington to the trail is not recommended, due to rough road conditions. Drive west from Vt. 100 in West Wardsboro. Signs to Stratton and Arlington mark the turn. After 5.2 miles you'll see

Stratton Mountain and Pond

46. Stratton Mountain and Pond

Time allowed: 2 days, 1 night
Class: II & III
Vertical rise: 1,981 feet
Distance (around loop): 13.2 miles
Hiking time: 7 hours

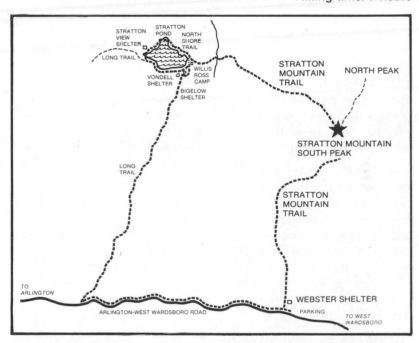

the blue sign for the Stratton Mountain Trail on the right. Just before the trail a small opening on the right leads to adequate off-the-road parking.

This rather rocky trail soon leads past Webster Shelter at .1 miles. The structure was named for Daniel Webster, who delivered a campaign speech nearby in 1840. At that time, Stratton Mountain rose above one of the most prosperous lumbering and agricultural districts of the state. The Stratton Turnpike added to the area's distinctiveness; it was the road taken by Boston's "best citizens" enroute to summer vacations at Saratoga Springs.

This prestigious area was selected as the site for a large Whig campaign rally for Harrison and Tyler. A fifty-by-one-hundred-foot log cabin was constructed just off the highway, to house the gathering. With Daniel Webster as the orator, the gathering drew a crowd of 15,000 persons (the exact count has been questioned, however, because of the tremendous amounts of hard cider that flowed throughout the proceedings).

Beyond the shelter, the trail forks. Go left on the blue-blazed Stratton Mountain Trail.

Trickling water wets the path as it winds upward at a moderate grade through many evergreens. Telephone lines accompany the way from time to time.

Bear left at the fork after .5 miles. Beyond this point the path follows a long, direct rise up the side of a hill. The way slides between giant rocks as it leads upward.

Continuing through hardwoods, this well-marked and cleared trail passes just beneath the ridge line on the west side of the slope;

then it cuts across the ridge to the east side and bends left. At 1.7 miles, it follows an arrow and makes a sharp swing up to the right.

After a short, steep section, the way resumes its moderate pitch. Grasses and wood asters flourish in open areas. The path crosses a brook at 2 miles and turns right, just beyond. Telephone lines go left here.

Rougher and steeper, the trail carves its way up through more evergreens. At 2.2 miles a grassy

Stratton Mountain

trail forks to the left. Continue straight on the Stratton Mountain Trail.

You emerge onto an old trail at 2.3 miles. Directly ahead a comfortable log bench (the work of some thoughtful person) is situated at just the right spot and welcomes your use.

You reach the summit of Stratton Mountain after a climb of 2.5 miles. Two small buildings and a fire tower occupy this area. Fantastic views await you from the top of the tower. The panorama is unusual, because you are able to see some of the more famous peaks from angles which isolate them against the horizons.

Equinox Mountain, highest of the Taconic Range, is to the west. Northeast is Mount Ascutney. New Hampshire's Mount Monadnock dominates the southeastern skyline. South is Somerset Reservoir and Mount Snow. Glastenbury Mountain rises in the southwestern corner.

Beyond and to the left of the tower, the blue-blazed Stratton Mountain Trail descends from the summit. Water seeps onto the path, making the way black and mirey. The grade shortly becomes more gradual as the

trail winds down through open woods. After crossing a fast-flowing brook at 3.8 miles, the descent becomes even more gentle.

Beside the trail at 4.1 miles are the remains of an old log camp. Giant moss-green logs lie in a tumble to the right of the path.

Another ½ mile of hiking takes you across a slow-running brook to a beaver pond. Crossing another stream, you can watch its waters flow into yet another pond on the right. As the trail angles left, take time to look for the beaver lodge at the back of this pond.

After winding along above this pond, the way dips down to meet an old road. Swing left onto it.

Follow the road as it passes through the tall grass of open fields, and over several streams. With the passage of time this open setting will become a forest landscape. At the 5-mile point, branch left at the fork and leave the road. Almost immediately you make an angled swing to the right.

Shortly before winding down to Stratton Pond, the path travels near another beaver pond. At 5.5 miles you reach the trail

junction at the pond's shore. Go right on the North Shore Trail. This path edges close to the waters of Stratton Pond for most of its length. Soon you pass a short spur on the right leading to a primitive camping area.

The North Shore Trail swings sharply left across a long tree, which forms a sturdy footbridge. A seemingly endless tangle of roots must then be maneuvered over and around. More sun-bleached logs carry you across boggy areas. Soon good views of Stratton Mountain open back across the pond. The lower north peak is to the left; the higher south peak with its fire tower is to the right.

At 6.2 miles you reach Stratton View Shelter. The mountain fills the skyline across the pond. A Green Mountain Club caretaker collects a fee (members 50¢; non-members 75¢) for overnight use of this three-sided, dirt-floored shelter.

Vondell and Bigelow Shelters are .3 and .5 miles further on. Although their settings do not have Stratton View's appeal, they do offer the added luxury of a floor.

Stratton Mountain

Second Day

Stratton View Shelter to Arlington-West Wardsboro Road

Class: II
Vertical rise: 365 feet
Distance: 7 miles
Hiking time: 3½ hours

To make your stay at Stratton View Shelter worthwhile, get up early today. Allow plenty of time for enjoying this scenic spot. You might see early morning animal activity close to the pond's edges. If the weather cooperates, you'll greet the sun as it rises over the mountain and paints the pond red.

Birds hopping about at bush level are certain to catch your eye. The dark-eyed junco will be feeding on seeds, weeds, or caterpillars and other insects. This bird is used to hikers around the shelter and is quite tame. The grey male has white outer tail feathers. The brown-backed female resembles the sparrow.

When ready to depart, take the North Shore Trail to the right. It passes over several boggy areas as it follows the pond's shore line.

After .1 miles you reach an intersection filled with many signs.

Follow the white blazes of the Long Trail south to the pond's shore. It goes left and cuts across the Stratton Pond outlet via long logs wired together.

On land again, the path winds through very damp areas. Long series of walkalongs provide firmer footing. Tangled roots lace the trail whenever you step on hard ground.

At .3 miles you come to the Vondell Shelter. The International Paper Company constructed this lean-to in 1967. It has bunk space for six to eight hikers.

The trail continues along the water's edge to the Bigelow Shelter at .5 miles. This lean-to sleeps six in bunks and might be an alternate stopping place—if you should camp in this area during a busy weekend.

Continuing its water-edge route, the trail enters a clearing at .7 miles. Just beyond is Willis Ross Camp. This structure can sleep twelve and has a spring 30 feet to the north.

From the clearing follow the sign for the Long Trail south to the right. Leaving the pond behind, climb gradually up over a mixture of rocks and roots.

A sign announcing the distance

to the Arlington-West Wardsboro Road stops the trail at .8 miles. The way swings sharply right here and begins a bumpy journey. It dips in spots, but remains fairly level. Crossing a small brook at 1.4 miles, the way turns left.

After a gradual climb the trail levels off again. The thin woods are filled with ferns and shining club moss. Needles cover the trail as you begin to wander through spruces and balsam firs.

There is little change in elevation as the trail log-hops over boggy areas and twists between evergreens. Frequent short dips and rises hinder you from maintaining a steady stride. Don't just pass by the damp boggy areas. These are prime spots for finding animal tracks. Deer, bear, raccoon, bobcat, porcupine—any of these animals might have passed this way recently.

Many older, dead trees have visible holes in their trunks. Made either by woodpeckers or branches breaking off, they provide homes for tree swallows, chickadees, nuthatches, wrens, bluebirds, squirrels, raccoons, and martens.

Stratton Mountain

Topping a short slope, the path becomes alternately smooth and rocky. It dips down a short steep bank and spans a large, boggy area atop logs.

At 2.3 miles the trail crosses an old grassy road and bears left. After a gradual climb it becomes flatter, smoother, and muddier.

Beginning a long series of bends and straightaways, the trail passes through unchanging woods. This area provides opportunities to do several things while walking along. Try brushing up on tree identification. Many of the hardwoods common to New England fill these woods.

At the 4-mile point the trail diagonally crosses an old road. It proceeds gradually downward over squishy terrain. Leveling out, the way swings sharply right and drops down to the Arlington-West Wardsboro Highway.

Turn left onto the dirt road (it changes to tar farther on). From here you have a 2.7-mile walk back to your car. Unlike the quick dips and rises of the trail, the smoothness of the road will let you stretch your leg muscles. You'll be able to set a good pace from here on.

Stratton Mountain

47. Middlebury Gap to Brandon Gap

Time allowed: 2 days, 1 night
Class: III & IV
Vertical rise: 2,535 feet
Distance (one way, no return hike): 9.8 miles
Hiking time: 7½ hours

Sucker Brook Shelter

Cape Lookoff Mountain sign

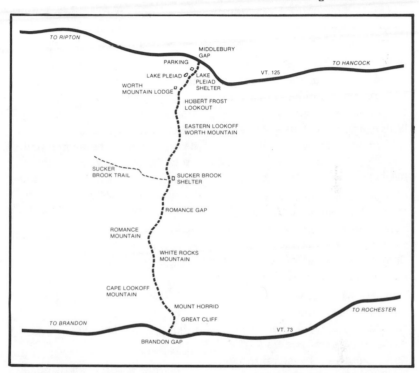

You'll hike up and down five different peaks with continuing panoramas highlighting the way during this two-day trip. There will be plenty of time for stops at the many lookoffs along the trail.

In 1915 Colonel Joseph Battell, an early spokesman for conservation of Vermont's forests, bequeathed to Middlebury College most of the land this hike passes over. At a time (late 1800s) when his friends were paying thousands of dollars for paintings, Battell bought thousands of acres of land for from ten to fifty cents an acre. As the rates rose, he bought hundreds more at $1.25 per acre.

Responsibility for maintaining this section of the Long Trail (your route for the hike) rests with the U.S. Forest Service. The Middlebury College Mountain Club, however, does the actual work. The trail is extremely well-marked, easy to follow, and well-cleared of debris.

First Day

Brandon Gap to Robert Frost Lookout, Worth Mountain, and Sucker Brook Shelter

Class: III

Vertical rise; 1,420 feet
Distance: 4.4 miles
Hiking time: 3½ hours

To reach Middlebury Gap, drive 6.4 miles west from Hancock or 5.6 miles east from Ripton on the Robert Frost Memorial Drive (Vt. 125). The brown and yellow "Long Trail—Green Mountain National Forest" sign on the north side of the road is the landmark to watch for. Across the highway is a large parking area. (You'll finish this hike about eight miles due south at Vt. 73; remember to arrange for transportation back to your car.)

From the south side of Vt. 125 climb up the white-blazed Long

Trail into the woods. The grade quickly eases as the thin tree cover stretches outward.

A ski slope appears through scattered trees to the left, as the path parallels another slope on the right. Continuing moderately upward, the trail crosses intersecting ski slopes and enters the woods beyond. White markers clearly show the way.

The grade becomes more gradual and the walking easier. Suddenly the trail drops and makes a long descent to Lake Pleiad Shelter. You have come .3 miles from Middlebury Gap.

A white arrow guides you past the shelter's left side. Cross an open ski slope and enter the woods again. The trail flattens out as it passes through thick stands of birches and striped maples and a gathering of spruces.

Long logs carry you across a brook as you approach a trail intersection. The blue-blazed spur to Lake Pleiad exits straight ahead. Turn sharply left on the Long Trail.

As the pitch increases the path becomes rougher. Leveling out, the trail intersects an old logging road. Watch carefully for

the white markers. Cross diagonally to the right, and back into the woods.

Rising steeply, the path crosses two ski trails. From the sloping ledge on the second trail it turns sharply right and zig zags up a steep, roughly cleared slope. At its crest, follow the beaten path up to the left. It quickly joins with the blue-blazed spur leading right to Worth Mountain Lodge. Bear left with the Long Trail.

The way continues upward to the Robert Frost Lookout. The sloping hillside opens up before you and offers spectacular views to the northeast. Mountains near and far seem to roll upon each other like gentle waves.

After a short, moderate climb the path flattens out. It winds cozily through stands of trail-hugging evergreens. With the flatness comes wetness. Boggy areas must be gingerly negotiated.

After dropping over smooth ledge, the dirt path begins a long, moderate ascent over occasional ledge and roots. The aroma of spruce and balsam enlivens your senses. Partial views of nearby mountains are available through thin trees to the left.

A slight descent is followed by more level, boggy areas. Beginning another climb, the path rises steeply over ledge and clinging roots. At 2.5 miles it enters the small clearing at Eastern Lookoff. The elevation here is 3,230 feet. Neighboring peaks sit atop one another as they stretch into the distance.

Another .1 mile brings you to the top of Worth Mountain, elevation 3,300 feet. The heavily wooded summit offers no views.

During the long, steep descent from Worth Mountain, you have continuous panoramic views of the Green Mountains stretching southward. Killington Peak is particularly prominent.

This entire section of the Long Trail is a haven for partridge. If you are lucky, you might surprise this wise game bird atop a stump or rock while it performs its strutting, spring courtship ritual. More probably, some of them will see you first and rocket upward through thick tree branche You will often hear the powerful beating of their wings, but never see them at all.

The path levels out after its descent from Worth Mountain. It follows a series of dips and rises and begins a long, gradual descent through thinned-out woods.

Dropping down over a short ledge, the way swings left through a stand of beeches. These stately trees seem to improve with age. The smooth, light grey bark gives them an elegance lacking in their rougher-barked companions.

Hardwood forests flank the path as it rises moderately. Glacial boulders become prominent, and shoulder-high spruces edge the trail as the hillside slopes steeply away.

At 4.3 miles the trail crosses a brook flowing quickly down the sloping hill. The Sucker Brook Shelter is just beyond at 4.4 miles. Its green floor can easily sleep six to eight hikers. Water is available just to the south where Sucker Brook passes under the Long Trail.

Second Day

Sucker Brook Shelter to Romance, White Rocks, and Cape Lookoff mountains, Mount Horrid and the Great Cliff, and Vt. 73.

Class: IV
Vertical rise: 1,115 feet
Distance: 5.4 miles
Hiking time: 4 hours

Leaving Sucker Brook Shelter, remember to fill your water containers at the brook. Ahead of you today is some steady trekking to four summits and, finally, a rugged descent from the Great Cliff of Mount Horrid.

A short way south of Sucker Brook Shelter, the Long Trail intersects with the Sucker Brook Trail. This blue-blazed trail leads west down the valley to the Ripton-Goshen Road. Stay on the Long Trail.

Making its way to Romance Mountain, the path leads through Romance Gap. Twisting and turning, it climbs steeply over rocks and roots. After cresting this long slope, the path levels out. Shining club moss gleams against the brownish-red carpet of evergreen spills.

A delicious aroma engulfs you as the trail passes through darkened groves of conifers. After more climbing between moss-covered rocks and logs, you emerge onto the eastern summit of Romance Mountain (1.4 miles from Sucker Brook Shelter). There is no view from the tree-covered top of this 3,020-foot peak.

Swing left; the way drops down off the summit. Very shortly, you

come to a fork where a 50-foot spur leads to an eastern overlook. As you continue south on the Long Trail a view to the west also appears.

Walkalongs aid you through this jumbled area of twisting trail, logs, and roots. This section of the trail follows the ridge line. However, views to the east and west are screened by stands of trees. Occasional spurs lead left and right off the path to overlook areas.

After 2.2 miles the narrow ledged trail leads upward to the 3,307-foot summit of White Rocks Mountain. From this vantage point you can look to the north and see Romance Mountain. As you begin the descent, green waves of mountains roll south and westward.

The steep way down over rough sections becomes fairly level and proceeds through fir forests. The path moves gradually upward over patches of ledge to another small clearing where a sign marks the 3,298-foot summit of Cape Lookoff Mountain. A short spur leads west from this heavily-treed summit, to an overview.

Leaving Cape Lookoff, you wind

your way down over more ledged areas. Continue more gradually downward through stands of birches surrounded by leafy ferns. Then, going up over roots and rocks, you begin a sustained ascent to 3,150-foot Mount Horrid. From here you can look back to Cape Lookoff Mountain and enjoy your recent accomplishment.

The descent from Mount Horrid is a rough one over steep areas of jumbled rock. Walkalongs provide welcome support across particularly boggy areas. There is flatter walking through an area of gnarled birches just before your arrival at the Mount Horrid Lookoff sign (4.8 miles from the start of the day's hiking). Caution rules here. The cliff face drops sharply off and falls six hundred feet to the gap below. Vt. 73 looks like a slender ribbon as it winds through Brandon Gap. Above it, the Green Mountain chain stretches southward.

Returning from the cliff, go left and follow the white blazes down to Brandon Gap. This .6-mile descent is extremely precipitous in places. It drops very steeply over ledge and roots before it levels out. The sides along the entire descent route are forested with sparkling paper birches.

The trail becomes more gradual. After a final easy descent, you emerge from the woods and walk through shrubbery and grass to Vt. 73. To the east, Rochester and Vt. 100 are 9.7 miles away; to the west, Brandon and U.S. 7 are 8.2 miles distant.

Middlebury Gap to Brandon Gap

48. The Coolidge Range

Time allowed: 3 days, 2 nights
Class: III & IV
Vertical rise: 4,693 feet
Distance (one way; no return hike): 16.7 miles
Hiking time: 12 hours

Hiking on the Long Trail

This backpacking trip takes you (principally on the Long Trail) through the northern mountains of the Coolidge Range. Two of Vermont's most popular peaks are the main attractions here. Pico Peak (elevation 3,957 feet) raises its cone-shaped dome high above Sherburne Pass. Killington Peak (elevation 4,241 feet), second highest in Vermont, is the more pointed mountain to the south of Pico.

Most of the steep climbing will be done during the first day and a half. During the second half of this trip, continuous downhill walking puts more strain on the knees than the thighs. You'll have plenty of time for scenery gazing without having to be concerned about hiking time.

First Day

Sherburne Pass to Pico Peak, Pico Camp, and Cooper Lodge

Class: IV

Vertical rise: 3,287 feet
Distance: 5.8 miles
Hiking time: 4½ hours

The Long Trail crossing at Sherburne Pass marks the beginning of your hike. Follow U.S. 4

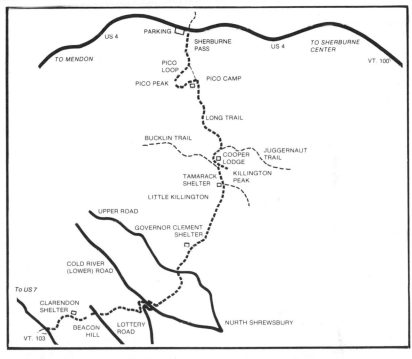

east from Rutland or west from Sherburne Center, to the height-of-land. The Long Trail Lodge is just west of the Long and Appalachian trail signs here. There is off-the-road parking on the south side of the highway. (This trip ends at Rt. 103 in East Clarendon. You'll have to make plans to return to your car from that point.)

Follow the white blazes south. Don't be fooled by the northward loop. The trail quickly begins

a gradual, southerly climb between glacial boulders.

After about 500 feet you reach a trail sign. It is 2.4 miles to the top of Pico from here. The grade becomes moderately steep as you swing sharply left. Stones fill the path, making the footing less certain.

The trail passes a variety of topographical features as it continues its steady upward climb. The path gouges into the earth before climbing over roots and ledge. Many spindly young trees fill the woodlands. Two huge glacial boulders, both supporting colonies of moss and several trees, are passed on the left. After a looping S-turn, the way widens and crosses damp, muddy areas.

Partridge thrive all through this section. It's exciting to hear their whirring wings and see the blurred shadows disappearing beyond thick branches. But seeing the small, tufted head and wide, fan-shaped tail close-up is really breath-taking.

The climb from Sherburne Pass has led diagonally upward. At .6 miles the trail crests the low ridge, swings up to the left, and becomes more moderate. As it passes along the east side of the ridge, the pitch lessens still more.

Ferns dominate the forest floor, as you pass through yellow and white birches. The trail crosses to the west side of the ridge line. Through scattered openings in the now-intermingling white birches and evergreens, you catch glimpses of Pico Peak up ahead.

Sink Brook is on the right side

at 1.1 miles. Swing left over ledge to the east side of the ridge again.

Cut logs help you over a brook at 1.2 miles. Swinging right, the trail begins a long, steady climb. Evergreens predominate, as you walk through and beneath their spreading limbs.

At 1.8 miles you emerge onto a ski slope. Proceed upward along its left edge for about 500 feet to Pico Junction. It is now .6 miles to the summit of Pico Peak via Pico Loop.

Continue straight up the ski slope for 100 feet and follow the blue blazes into the woods. The trail now gets very rough. It narrows between body-brushing branches. Twisting and turning, it courses up over rocks, roots, and ledge. Evergreen smells sweeten this primitive path.

Three ski trails are crossed before the way leads beneath the Pico Chair Lift. Ahead to the right is a wide, bare path leading to the summit. Microwave towers welcome you at the top. Primary views extend to the north and south. Killington Peak fills the area to the southwest.

On leaving the summit, retrace your previous route under the

lift and bear right down the ski slope. Blue blazes will guide you through a line of trees on the right. Walk through them onto the road, and down 50 feet to the blaze on the right.

A narrow, winding, sometimes-steep descent of .4 miles brings you to Pico Camp. Built in 1959, this frame cabin has bunks for twelve people. From the clearing here you look south to Killington Peak and southeast to Mount Ascutney. This is the halfway point of today's hike and a good spot to rest awhile. A spring is located 100 feet to the north on the Long Trail.

Below to the right the Long Trail South begins a very long, gradual descent. For approximately 1 mile you hike along the west side of the ridge and enjoy the gradual ups and downs in the trail. One heavily-rooted section offers the only change from the surprisingly comfortable going.

At 3.9 miles a steeper descent leads to a raised walkalong. Boggy areas lie ahead. Rocks and logs help you through them. You pass a .3 mile spur trail to Ram's Head Mountain on the left as the path returns to its level grade.

Coolidge Range

Killington looms ahead. At 4.3 miles a sign informs you that you are now halfway between Pico Camp and Cooper Lodge. Only 1½ miles left today.

The Long Trail recently has been relocated to the west side of Snowden Peak. Signs mark both ends of the change. No longer does the trail pass by the Snowden lifts. Enjoy the uninterrupted wilderness walking.

Your first noticeable climb since leaving Pico Camp begins at the northern end of the new route. The grade rises steeply over rivers of rocks and flattens out only occasionally along this revised section.

Approaching the Killington West Glade Ski Trail, the path swings right. Rocks and crusty roots make the footing wobbly. Several small brooks and walkalongs are crossed before an iron pipe drips spring water onto the trail at 5.7 miles.

The Juggernaut Trail joins from the left at 5.8 miles. Cooper Lodge is just ahead.

This attractive shelter was constructed in 1939 by the Vermont Forest Service and extensively repaired in 1969 by the Vermont Department of Forests and Parks. The floor and most of the walls are stone. A picnic table, stove, and bunk space for twelve to sixteen will make you comfortable tonight. Springs are located 100 feet south of the lodge.

Second Day

Cooper Lodge to Killington Peak, Consultation Point, and Governor Clement Shelter

Class: III
Vertical rise: 610 feet
Distance: 4.5 miles
Hiking time: 3½ hours

This day will include an ascent to Killington Peak. (The town that was once its namesake is today known as Sherburne.)

A vast 360-degree view from Killington's summit is sure to impress you. Ascutney rises most prominently to the southeast. The White Mountains of New Hampshire are visible in the northeast. To the west are Mendon Peak, the City of Rutland, Lake Champlain, and the Adirondacks of New York State. You look down on the summit of Pico Peak to the north.

From Cooper Lodge take the Long Trail South. Follow its white blazes approximately 100 feet to a small clearing. Here the blue-blazed spur to Killington Peak leads east off the Long Trail.

This .2-mile spur to the summit is a steep climb over jagged pieces of rock and ledge. Scrub growth edges the trail.

Your first view of the top includes a lookout tower (not open to the public) and a radio installation. A spur to the east takes you to the Killington Gondola Terminal and Restaurant.

When ready to resume your backpacking journey, descend to the Long Trail via the Killington Peak spur and go left (south).

The path follows an easy grade along the southwest slope. It is possible to maintain a smooth and spirited stride over this undemanding section of trail. Spruce and balsam spills give the path its "bounciness."

At .8 miles from the start of today's hike the way begins an extended gradual descent. There's a quietness about this evergreen-rimmed path. Kneel to examine the clover-like clumps of wood sorrel. On an autumn morning their three-part compound leaves may be delicately outlined by frost. Chickadees abound.

Near a clump of wood sorrel there may be a group of "creeping evergreens." Shining club moss is the species that predominates here. Tiny, bright-green, pointed leaves encircle its erect stalks.

A gradual descent over a rocky path leads you to Tamarack Shelter spur after 1½ miles. (A sign and the short spur trail lead right to it. To the left the blue-blazed Shrewsbury Trail goes southeast toward Shrewsbury Peak.) Continue on the white-blazed Long Trail. The path maintains its gentle trend as it crosses the east slope of Little Killington. At 1.8 miles you reach Consultation Point, elevation 3,750 feet.

After leaving Consultation Point, the trail slices along the south slope of Little Killington. It becomes narrower and very rough as it winds around trees and over roots and rocks. To the left, the hillside slopes off steeply. Ever so slowly, you make your way downhill.

After crossing two small streams, the Long Trail swings sharply right at 2.6 miles. It becomes an easy, level walk once again.

Oak and beech are prominent in the deciduous forest to the sides of the path.

Such open woods as these are the blue jay's favored habitat.

This handsome bird has an assortment of voices, ranging from raucous calls to melodious warbles. Blue jays include insects in their summer diet, but are primarily vegetarians. Interestingly, they perform an important reforestation service. By burying more acorns and beechnuts than they ever can eat, they help plant new trees.

About ½ mile from the last sharp turn, you cross a walk-along and turn sharply left onto an old road. Very quickly, you turn right off this road and continue on a path twisting through open woods.

Soon the trail crosses a road. It proceeds downward through more woods and emerges onto still another old road. It follows this awhile before branching right onto a rocky, gutted path.

At 4.2 miles this trail descends some sturdy log stairs and joins an old logging road. Follow it to the right.

A rushing brook parallels the

way on the left. Ahead you can see the roof of the Governor Clement Shelter. The trail winds left to a junction. A spur leads left to the brook and another swings right toward the stone shelter where you'll spend the night.

The William H. Field family of Mendon erected this shelter in 1929. It bears the name of Percival W. Clement, who governed Vermont from 1919 to 1921. Its deep-set bunks accommodate eight to ten persons. A picnic table and stone fireplace add luxury to the comfortable setting.

Third Day

Clement Shelter to Beacon Hill and Vt. 103

Class: III
Vertical rise: 790 feet
Distance: 6.4 miles
Hiking time: 4 hours

Two steep climbs to hilltops interrupt, and add diversity to, today's long, gradual descent. The walking is easy; you will have time to enjoy this leisurely hike.

From the shelter, descend to the road and turn right. Running water becomes audible on both sides. After .4 miles the left stream flows under a road bridge and joins with the stream on the right.

Another bridge appears at a wide bend in the road after .6 miles. Follow the white arrow into the evergreens just before the bridge. The flat trail dips down to the edge of the roaring stream.

The steep hillside closes down to the path. Step carefully over the slippery roots along this very narrow part of the trail.

Yellow birches lead into evergreens as the path swings away from the water. Enjoy the flat, winding path through these thick trees. Upper Road interrupts the tranquility at 1.2 miles—but only until you re-enter the woods on the other side.

The trail continues flat and narrow. It crosses several small brooks and many boggy areas. Few logs or walkalongs aid your travel in these muddy sections. Look to the sides of the trail for the firmest footing.

Much of the path is sandy as you continue within sound of the stream. The path winds along next to the water again. Such airy openness offers a nice change from the narrow, tree-lined trail.

Rising steeply from the water's edge, the way leads over a hogback. It's a little like walking over a natural bridge. Streams rush by far below on both sides, as the straight path passes beneath towering evergreens.

The trail drops down to a dry brook bed and follows it to a junction with a wide stream. Pick your route and rock-hop across.

Switch back to the left and climb steeply up away from the stream. Pass through the open field filled with goldenrod, ferns, and wood asters. An old stone wall guards your entrance back into the woods.

More boggy areas are crossed before the Long Trail forks right at 2.7 miles. Just ahead is a white sign, author unknown. It reads: "Long Trail—the longest river in Vermont."

A mobile home and garage appear on the right. Keep left on the gravel road leading to the next mobile home on the left. Enter the woods again at the white arrow on the right and continue past yet another mobile home out onto Cold River (Lower) Road. Go right.

Take the first left onto a gravel

Along the Long Trail

road and follow its uphill route. A white arrow (3.2 miles from Clement Shelter) guides you back into the woods to the right.

A long, steady climb brings you to the top of the ridge. You're very likely to see golden-crowned kinglets anywhere along here. These tiny (three-to-five-inch) birds are a dull, olive-grey color, with golden crowns bordered by black and white. They can be seen feeding on branches of firs, spruces, or other conifers. Like the black-capped chickadee, they will often fly close to look you over.

The way descends from the ridge and passes over more boggy

areas, before reaching the trail register and Hermit Spring at 4.3 miles. During dry seasons, though, water may not be available here.

Just after crossing the corner of a rocky pasture, the path winds through some unusual trees. These tamaracks (American larches) are northern conifers which shed their leaves in the fall. Short needles grow in tufts at the ends of abbreviated branches, and give the tree a spidery look. Tiny, scaly cones sit upright. Its tough root fibers were used by eastern Indians to bind birch bark canoe seams. Grouse, hares, red squirrels, porcupines and deer eat the seeds, needles, and inner bark.

The trail passes through the pasture again and crosses Lottery Road at 4.7 miles. It ascends steeply over rocks and smooth ledge to Beacon Hill. The elevation of this grassy knoll is 1,740 feet. Keep to the left of the signed telephone pole and begin the steep, winding descent.

Long thorns are the first clue to another group of unusual trees. Hawthorns are small trees or shrubs with long thorns and smooth, brown bark which breaks into thin, scaly plates

with age. Their small yellow-red fruit is often available throughout winter, and provides food for numerous birds and mammals. Songbirds prefer these trees for nesting because of the dense cover the hawthorn's branches offer.

The rocky descent culminates

at Clarendon Shelter after 5.6 miles. The trail passes left of the shelter through the cleared area, and swings right to a stone wall. Step over it onto the dirt road and go left. This flat road bears right at a fork and leads .8 miles to Vt. 103, where your backpacking trip terminates.

Coolidge Range

49. The Presidential Range: Lincoln Gap to Middlebury Gap

Time allowed: 3 days, 2 nights
Class: III & IV
Vertical rise: 4,457 feet
Distance (one way; no return hike): 17.7 miles
Hiking time: 13 hours

Each of the eight mountains included in this north-to-south trip rises over three thousand feet (the highest is 3,823 feet). From their summits and trails you'll see the New Haven River Basin with its semi-circle of towering peaks, the massive Champlain Valley, and a vast variety of mountains. Among this quiet splendor you'll bed down just above an isolated pond high on a mountainside. To enjoy all this to the fullest, make sure you've limbered up any rusty muscles well in advance.

This backpacking journey takes you over "Presidential peaks" from the Lincoln-Warren Highway to Vt. 125. The U.S. Forest Service does an excellent job of maintaining the trails. They are free from windfalls and obstructions. Short logs corduroy wet sections of the trail, giving firmer footing. Over very damp, boggy areas, rough-hewn logs have been extended lengthwise to form narrow foot bridges.

First Day

Lincoln Gap to Mount Grant and Cooley Glen Shelter

Birch roots

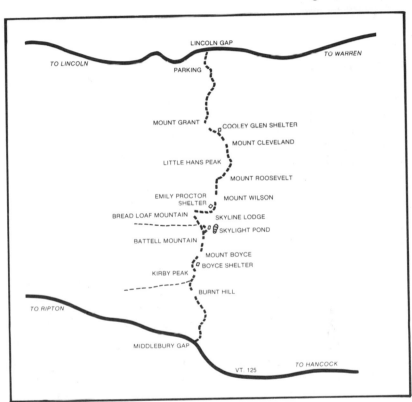

Class: III
Vertical rise: 1,916 feet
Distance: 4.6 miles
Hiking time: 3½ hours

The access road for this trip is the Lincoln-Warren Highway. Drive from either Lincoln or Warren to the height-of-land. A brown and yellow "Long Trail-Green Mountain National Forest" sign marks the 2,410-foot elevation of Lincoln Gap. Ample off-the-road parking is available here. (You'll have to work out a way back to your car when the hike ends at Vt. 125.)

On the southern side of the highway, follow the white blazes up the embankment. The slope steepens almost immediately. Lacking the switchbacks which will ease the approach to Mount Grant, this climb presents the most rugged vertical rise of the day.

The steeply sloping trailsides are forested with birches, beeches, and maples. At .6 miles you come to a flat-ledged area which offers limited views of southern peaks. Most prominent in the panorama before you is Mount Grant. To the west, you can look across Lake Champlain and see the Adirondacks in the distance.

Descend from this smooth open ledge into the woods. Occasional clusters of fern fill the forest to either side.

Infrequent sections of ledge and loose rock cross the packed dirt trail. After the initial steep climb, it proceeds more gently over small drops and rises and long, flat stretches.

As the path rambles through one such level section, it passes beneath a monstrous old birch tree. Twelve-to-fourteen feet in circumference, it leans its mass across the trail at a 30-degree angle, resembling the elongated barrel of a great cannon.

Rougher footing marks a series of switchbacks. Further on, cut logs provide traction as the path leads over level areas of black mud and across a ridge.

A small tumbling brook begins to parallel the trail. At 2.6 miles you cross it via two sturdy, rough-hewn logs. The trail continues to wind its way upward along the west ridge of Mount Grant and shortly crosses to the east.

Picking your way over loose rocks and tangles of roots, you climb up the steep east ridge. Intermittent views of near and far mountains appear between the trees. Needles carpet the way as the delicious aroma of spruce and balsam engulfs you.

After ascending areas of packed dirt and ledge sandwiched between shorter evergreens, you emerge onto level ledge: the summit of Mount Grant, elevation 3,661 feet.

Signs direct you to the right for a close vista which includes Mounts Cleveland, Roosevelt, and Wilson and Bread Loaf Mountain. Beyond, to the south and southeast, are Killington Peak and Mount Ascutney.

It is .7 miles from here to the Cooley Glen Shelter. Your descent south from the summit begins steeply. It drops over long sections of smooth ledge and loose rock between stands of trail-hugging evergreens. Nimble stepping is needed around and down over these areas of ledge. Directly ahead, Mount Cleveland comes into full view.

The trail becomes wetter as the grade lessens. At one point it veers sharply left around a particularly boggy area. Cut logs aid your passage over wet, muddy sections.

Soon the path becomes very gradual and, eventually, level. Packed dirt replaces the rocks and roots, making for easier walking. The way widens, and continues through a great stand of fir and spruce to Cooley Glen Shelter.

This frame lean-to, erected in 1965 by the U.S. Forest Service, has room for six to eight people and will see you through your first night. Branching right from the Long Trail South just beyond the shelter, the Cooley Glen Trail leads 500 feet to a spring.

Second Day

Cooley Glen Shelter to Mounts Cleveland, Roosevelt, Wilson,

Bread Loaf Mountain, and Skyline Lodge

Class: IV

Vertical rise: 1,966 feet
Distance: 7.8 miles
Hiking time: 6 hours

As you can see from a check of
the distance, this will be a full
day of hiking. Much of it is up
and down an assortment of peaks.
You'll want to be well rested
and get an early start.

Leaving Cooley Glen Shelter,
the Long Trail South climbs
very steeply upward to the east.
Twisting and turning, the path

Massive birch guards the Long Trail

becomes moderate and even
gradual as it passes through
stands of balsam and spruce.
The footing is rooted at times,
but rock-free.

After a quick ½ mile, you arrive
at the heavily wooded summit of
Mount Cleveland, elevation 3,500
feet. No views.

Descend gradually down along
the east ridge. A short climb
brings you across to the west
side. Descending again, you pass
through hundreds of handsome
white birches interspersed with
evergreens.

This long descent offers occasional views of the other peaks you'll
be visiting today. Stretching
southward before you are Mounts
Roosevelt, Wilson, and Bread
Loaf.

The contorted black skeletons
of aged, dead trees dot the lower
stretches of open woods. Their
rough, shingled bulks rise im-
posingly among the younger
surrounding trees. Shelves of
mushrooms and fungi thrive on
their surfaces.

The trail begins a moderate
climb. It flattens out again, then

Presidential Range

rises gradually and begins a long traverse to the east. Becoming steeper, it swings right and returns to the west side of the ridge line.

Crossing the ridge on a long, flat cut eastward, the path reaches the summit of Little Hans Peak at 2.1 miles. A wood sign gives the elevation as 3,400 feet.

Leading east from this summit, the path passes over occasional roots and a few rocks. Firs and spruces continue to perfume the air and spill needles on the trail.

At 2.4 miles from the beginning of the day's hiking, you cross a trickling brook. Climb easily upward to another long, wet, log-crossed area leading west. The trail winds back to the east and rises to a rocky overlook before crossing Mount Roosevelt's 3,580-foot summit. Descending in a southerly direction, Mount Wilson and Bread Loaf Mountain are visible at close range straight ahead.

The path gradually climbs, then drops. Step carefully over ledge and loose rocks as you go steeply downward. At the bottom of this slope the Clark Brook Trail leads left to Granville.

The trail now begins a long ascent to Mount Wilson. You wonder at times where the peak is, as the path descends over rocks and roots. Turning sharply left, the way scrambles moderately up over narrow ledge. Keeping to the east of the ridge, you make your way to the peak.

At the 4.8-mile point, you arrive at Mount Wilson, elevation 3,756 feet. The Long Trail leads to the right from this wooded summit. Before continuing, follow the short spur straight ahead for far-reaching views to the east and south.

Leaving Mount Wilson, the trail begins a short series of descents and ascents. It then starts a very long steep descent to Emily Proctor Shelter. Stepping down over precipitous sections of rocks and roots, you reach the shelter.

The Long Trail bears sharply left, crosses a brook, and passes upward over wet ground and rocks. At the 6.3-mile mark you enter a clearing containing a number of signs. The Long Trail makes a switchback left. Climb the right spur .1 miles to the vista on Bread Loaf Mountain. You'll want to spend some time enjoying the expansive view

across the Champlain Valley from this 3,823-foot vantage point.

Return to the clearing and proceed south. An interesting sign stops you after a short walk. Although probably not as meaningful to you as to a striving end-to-ender, it informs you that you are now at the midpoint of the Long Trail—equidistant (130.4 miles) from the Massachusetts and Canadian borders.

Step down over a damp path. Long, cut trees minimize the chances of sinking into the mud. Ledge marks the start of a very steep section.

Entering a clearing, the Skylight Pond Trail leads right toward Ripton. You are now only ¼ mile from Skyline Lodge. Continue straight for roughly 100 feet and turn left at the sign onto the Skylight Pond Trail. Follow the blue blazes to the lodge and pond.

This picturesque spot rewards your long day's hike. The lodge sits on a bluff overlooking Skylight Pond. From its raised porch you look across the tree-enclosed pond to distant peaks. With bunk and loft space for ten, plus water at a nearby spring, you should be quite comfortable here.

Presidential Range

Third Day

Skyline Lodge to Battell Mountain, Mount Boyce, Kirby Peak, Burnt Hill, and Middlebury Gap (Vt. 125)

Class: III

Vertical rise: 575 feet
Distance: 5.3 miles
Hiking time: 3½ hours

This last day of your backpacking trip offers an interesting assortment of hikes (over peaks), and visits to many overlooks.

Climb up the steep 500-foot trail behind Skyline Lodge to the brown-and-yellow sign directing you left to the Long Trail South. Go left and follow the white blazes.

After .2 miles on the Long Trail you pass over Battell Mountain. The elevation is 3,471 feet, but the heavily wooded summit does not provide any views.

Blister lichen abounds on evergreen bark. Its grey-green crust forms scaly patches on the dark bark. Varieties of moss also flourish. They form shiny green mats over ledge and on the forest floor. Wavy broom moss has long leaves with a silky shine. Indian brave moss has a tiny erect stalk from which two tiny leaves project like the feathers of a warrior's headband.

The gradual ups and downs of the trail frequently lead over boggy areas. Walkalongs aid your passage over these mirey sections.

After 1.2 miles the trail passes a sign to the right for the Boyce Lookout spur trail which leads 20 feet to a partial overlook to the west. A bit further, you cross over the wooded summit of 3,200-foot Mount Boyce.

The Long Trail makes a fairly long, gradual descent, reaching Boyce Shelter after about a mile's hike from Boyce summit.

The Long Trail resumes behind the shelter and rises steadily. It levels out and maintains a rough route over the rocks, slippery ledge, and roots of the west slope of Kirby Peak.

The Burnt Hill Trail joins with the Long Trail after another ¾ of a mile. This path, maintained by the Middlebury College Mountain Club, leads 6 miles to Ripton. A brown and yellow sign to your left points out that Middlebury Gap is ahead. Continue on the white-blazed Long Trail South.

At the 3.2-mile point in today's hike, after a short ascent, you reach the rounded, ledged area called Burnt Hill. There is a partial view over tree tops to the west. Follow the trail as it leads sharply left off the hill.

The now-gradual trail makes a long descent through thin forests. In the process it crosses the ridge from west to east. Occasional climbs over gnarled roots onto ledged areas vary the hiking. You eventually enter a small clearing where an unmarked spur trail leads left to an eastern vista.

Back on the main trail, pick your way around more boggy areas beyond the clearing. After descending a long, moderate slope you come to a sign pointing left to the Silent Cliff Trail. From the cliff there are views to Monastery and Middlebury gaps.

The Long Trail swings sharply right from this intersection and makes a long, steep descent. After leveling out, it rambles briefly through the woods before emerging onto a small embankment above Robert Frost Memorial Drive (Vt. 125) at Middlebury Gap.

Much folklore has been woven around the origin of Mount Mansfield—Vermont's highest peak. One tale has it that a chap named Mansfield was pitched off Camel's Hump when the beast stumbled while kneeling to drink. He lies, stone-faced, staring at the sky and giving the mountain its famous profile. Another story claims that it is the profile of Mishawaka, crippled son of an Indian chief, who perished on Mansfield's summit after crawling there to prove his courage and uphold his family's honor. Several stormy days followed his death, during which the mountained changed from one peak to the outline of Mishawaka's face.

There's a story about the naming of the mountain, too. The Abnaki Indians first christened it "Moze-o-de-be-Wado," meaning "Mountain-with-a-head-like-a-moose." Its present name though, is derived from that of the town (now Stowe) named formerly after the English Chief Justice, Lord Mansfield.

The following backpacking trip will take you to most of the mountain's famous points of interest. All the sections of its distinctive profile are included: Adam's Apple, Chin, Lower Lip, Upper Lip, Nose, and Forehead. You will also visit the Lake of the Clouds, Bear Pond, Cantilever Rock, and Wampahoofus Rock.

Our route is chosen from the system of trails which web Mount Mansfield. It includes the steepest half-mile of hiking trail in the state, as well as the highest point (the Chin, elevation 4,393 feet). Variety is provided by underpasses, switchbacks, crevices, caves, and ladder-and-cable climbing.

The trail system is maintained by the Green Mountain Club and the University of Vermont Outing Club. The G.M.C. cares for Taft and Butler lodges. Each of these sturdy log structures can accommodate up to sixteen hikers overnight. Fees are 50¢ for G.M.C. members and 75¢ for non-members.

First Day

Smugglers' Notch to "steepest half-mile in Vermont," Lake of the Clouds, Adam's Apple, and Taft Lodge

Class: V
Vertical rise: 1,920 feet
Distance: 2.3 miles
Hiking time: 3½ hours

The Bear Pond Trail rises out of Smugglers' Notch. The peaks of the Sterling and Worcester ranges, the Lake of the Clouds, and Mount Mansfield's Adam's Apple and Chin await the hiker who can meet this trail's challenge.

Make certain you are ready for this climb before starting out. Novice hikers have struggled up some of the steeper sections and reached the point where they could climb neither up nor down. Even experienced hikers find this trail a real challenge. The going is rugged and slippery in good weather, and downright dangerous in bad. If you are conditioned and experienced, your climb up the steepest half-mile of hiking trail in Vermont will be exhilarating.

To arrive at your starting point: drive north from Stowe on Vt. 108 past the Mansfield and Spruce Peak ski areas to Smugglers' Notch. The blue-blazed Bear Pond Trail leads west from the road at the notch's summit. Watch for a yellow road sign saying "Steep Winding Hill" and the blue blazes just beyond. There is a parking area on the east side of Route 108 diagonally across from the

50. Mount Mansfield

Time allowed: 5 days, 4 nights
Class: IV & V
Vertical rise: 7,080 feet
Distance (around loop): 17.1 miles
Hiking time: 18 hours

start of the Bear Pond Trail.
(You'll finish this backpacking
trip at the Gondola Parking
Area, just over 2 miles from
your car.)

Immediately, the trail starts
climbing up through clefts in
small boulders, twisting over
ledged areas. The gnarled roots
of tenacious birches and spruce
frequently provide the only footing as you scramble up these
near-vertical slopes. Hands and
feet search for these or any
other supports in the cracked
face of the ledge.

If you are carrying a medium-
to-heavy pack, remember to keep
leaning inward to maintain your
balance. A hiking stick can
provide much-needed leverage.

The trail skirts an overhanging
ledge directly above. Winding
around and mounting this ledge,
you'll be rewarded by your first
open view, east to the Sterling
Range and down into Smugglers'
Notch. Climbing higher, you'll
also be able to see the peaks of
the Worcester Mountains to the
southeast. An even more elevated
look to the left lets you see the
faded blue peaks of the White
Mountains on the horizon.

Thick evergreens cling to the

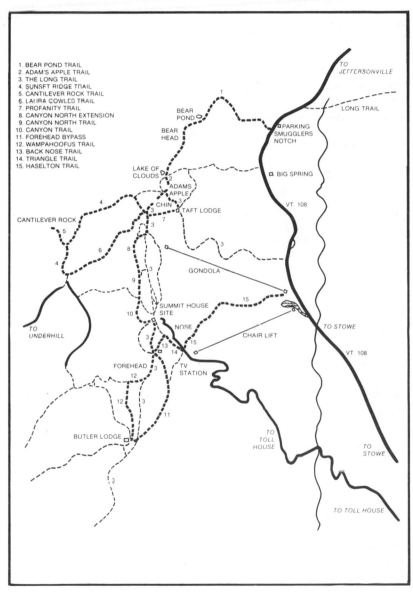

1. BEAR POND TRAIL
2. ADAM'S APPLE TRAIL
3. THE LONG TRAIL
4. SUNSET RIDGE TRAIL
5. CANTILEVER ROCK TRAIL
6. LAURA COWLES TRAIL
7. PROFANITY TRAIL
8. CANYON NORTH EXTENSION
9. CANYON NORTH TRAIL
10. CANYON TRAIL
11. FOREHEAD BYPASS
12. WAMPAHOOFUS TRAIL
13. BACK NOSE TRAIL
14. TRIANGLE TRAIL
15. HASELTON TRAIL

Mount Mansfield

edges of the trail. A trickle of water flows slowly down, wetting the ledge and roots and turning the dirt path to reddish-brown mud. The going can be very slippery. A woodsman's cup helps you collect enough water to quench your thirst.

Although roping over the rocks is not necessary, there are many particularly smooth, steep sections. You will need to stretch and grasp your way cautiously. The numerous medium-sized rocks which litter the path do not always offer sure footing.

After this steep, steady climb of ½ mile to the ridge, the hiking becomes less arduous. There are even occasional flat areas. But, here to greet you next are long series of black, muddy sections, alternating with still-steep rises in the trail. Logs can sometimes aid footing, but it is usually best—and driest—to walk around the edges of damp spots.

At .9 miles a short spur leads right to Bear Pond. This tiny mountain pond is well worth visiting. Its edges are surrounded by trees and rocks, giving it an aura of isolation.

Continuing along, the main trail again opens to striking views to the east. It eventually winds its way to the Lake of the Clouds. This is an area of fragile alpine vegetation. Walk carefully—and only on the path—to avoid disturbing the flora and fauna here.

After 1.8 miles the Bear Pond Trail ends at a 4-way intersection. The Hell Brook Trail enters from the left and continues across to the right. Go straight, following the Adam's Apple Trail. It climbs steeply .1 miles to the top of Mount Mansfield's Adam's Apple. Elevation here is 4,060 feet. From the open summit enjoy a close view south to the Chin and a pleasant look down upon the Lake of the Clouds. Turn west for a look at Lake Champlain, stretching for miles in the distance.

Continue on the Adam's Apple Trail. It is marked by a procession of cairns and blue blazes as it descends another .1 miles to meet the Hell Brook and Long trails at Eagle Pass.

Follow the blue blazes of the Long Trail North to the left. It slithers down over a spill of rocks paralleling a tiny stream. A hike of .3 miles brings you

to Taft Lodge, a thick-logged cabin with bunk space for sixteen persons, a toilet, and ample water supply. Spend your first night here.

Second Day

Taft Lodge Loop to the Chin and Cantilever Rock

Class: V
Vertical rise: 2,973 feet
Distance: 4.8 miles
Hiking time: 5¼ hours

With a good night's rest behind you and a hearty breakfast under your belt, you are now ready for today's trails. You'll pass over very little level ground. The way is all up and down steep grades, many of them wet and obstinate. Keep in mind, also, that most of the first half of the hike leads down, while the last portion is straight up.

Remember that the Laura Cowles Trail is very difficult, especially after you have climbed the Chin and descended the Sunset Ridge Trail. It is steep, exceptionally rocky, and extremely wet. The going is a rugged, slippery, one-step-at-a-time process most of the way. Conserve your energy for it. By the time you return to Taft Lodge at the end of the day

Lake of the Clouds

Mount Mansfield

you'll have earned a nourishing meal and a full night's sleep.

We recommend this particular route only to those who feel they are in strong physical condition. A great deal of previous hiking experience is not necessary—but stamina is. You don't want the steep return climb up the western slope to become so punishing that you are too exhausted to continue.

From Taft Lodge walk up the .3 miles on the Long Trail (which you descended yesterday) to the intersection of the Long, Adam's Apple, and Hell Brook trails. (From here it is .3 miles to the summit of the Chin, and another .2 miles down to the junction with the Sunset Ridge Trail.) Go left onto the Long Trail South.

The way leads up over boulders and ledge. It swings left around a sheer ledge face and up through a narrow crevice. Leading right, the path intersects with the Story Trail.

The climbing becomes steeper as you look almost straight up toward your goal. Swinging around to the north end of the ridge, you begin to realize how high up you are. It is often possible to see a clear blue sky above you, rolling waves of clouds below. Looking out across this ocean of thick, billowy whiteness, you can see occasional peaks emerging from the cloud cover.

Winding upward over lichen-covered ledge, you soon come to the summit, identified by a U.S. Geological Survey marker. This is the highest point in the state —the top of Vermont. Take time to enjoy both the feeling of accomplishment and the views from this unparalleled vantage point.

On a clear day you can see farther than you'd have thought possible. Looking north and a bit east you can see the Sterling Range, Cold Hollow Mountains, Belvidere Mountain, Big Jay, and Jay Peak. If the view is clear, you can see Mount Royal in Montreal just west of north. To the northeast are the Lake Willoughby mountains, Bald and Pisgah. Swinging east, you can clearly see the Worcester Mountains backed by the Granite Mountains.

South of east is Mount Washington in New Hampshire. The Franconia and Kinsman ranges— also in New Hampshire—extend farther south. The Green Mountains as far as Killington Peak are seen to the south, with Camel's Hump especially prominent. Southwest, you see Whiteface Mountain. Stretching for miles along the western horizon is Lake Champlain; behind it, the Adirondacks.

Follow the blazes (white-encircled-with-red) across the bare summit and down to the open grassy area. Here you'll see signs for the Long and Profanity trails. Continue on the Long Trail. Ahead is the junction of the Laura Cowles and Sunset Ridge trails. You have now come .8 miles from the shelter.

Go right onto the Sunset Ridge Trail. The path winds its way across the side of the ridge below the Chin. It passes over open ledge and down through scrub forest, eventually coming to the junction of the Story Trail. Stay on the Sunset Ridge Trail, go sharply left and begin descending the open ridge.

The descent begins gradually, over ledge and grass. Closely-grouped cairns and blue blazes guide your way. Endless trickles of water wet the ledges.

As you crest a small knoll (well down the ridge), turn to see where you have been. The Chin rises commandingly above everything in sight.

Trees increase in height as you descend from the scrub area and pass through leg-brushing balsam firs. The trail narrows, and tunnels downward through these taller trees. Cresting a small knoll you are engulfed by hordes of skeleton trees and then surrounded by shorter green ones.

The path swings sharply left past a huge submarine-shaped boulder. From here to its distant junction with the Cantilever Rock Trail, the Sunset Ridge Trail descends like a bobsled-run over sheer ledge. It narrows, twists, and slithers, as trees close in along the sides. Views are limited to the path directly in front of you. Ledges are steep and smooth. Water slickens much of the way. Footing is often best along the sides of the path where you can hold onto trees as you pick your way down. Full concentration is a must.

At the 2.2-mile point you come to the Cantilever Rock Trail. Follow this .2 miles to the right. You will cross three brooks and many roots, and skirt several boulders, before coming to Cantilever Rock.

The seventy-five-ton rock is forty feet long and extends thirty-one feet without support beyond the cliff's edge. Sixty feet up in the air, it protrudes like the narrow prow of a sailing ship. At other angles it looks like the bowsprit of a square-rigged brigantine. A log ladder invites you to climb up for a closer look.

Returning to the Sunset Ridge Trail, turn right. It joins .4 miles later with the Laura Cowles Trail. You cross several brooks via rocks and split-log bridges along the way. The trail becomes more gradual, and extremely wet. Walk over a footbridge to the wooden bench. The Laura Cowles Trail begins here. Go left.

This trail is marked by pale blue and occasional orange blazes. It follows and criss-crosses a brook for quite a distance. Becoming very steep, it continues even steeper as it climbs higher. A picturesque trail, it passes through thick stands of young trees.

At 3.9 miles the way seems to stop at a high, horizontally-ribbed ledge. Go right here if you have a pack. If not, you might want to try the steep spur to the left.

The path is extremely steep as it leads out over open ledge and intersects back with the Sunset Ridge Trail. Just ahead is the Profanity Trail which will lead you down a steep, rocky ½ mile back to Taft Lodge. This name might have been more appropriately applied to the Laura Cowles Trail, although it seems suitable here also.

Third Day

Taft Lodge to Butler Lodge

Class: IV
Vertical rise: 1,025 feet
Distance: 4.2 miles
Hiking time: 4½ hours

As indicated by the lower vertical rise, today's exploration of Mount Mansfield will not be as taxing as yesterday's. However, the trails require the agility and physical conditioning necessary to maneuver through and over a succession of narrow ledges, steep canyons, and rocky tunnels. Bring along water; there will be very little until you near Butler Lodge, where you'll spend the night.

Hike back up the Profanity Trail from Taft Lodge, ½ mile to its junction with the Long

Mount Mansfield

Trail South. You will gain a rapid 600 feet of elevation in this ½ mile.

Go left onto the Long Trail South. Follow the red-encircled white dots across open ledge splashed with green map lichen. Stay on the marked trail to avoid damaging the fragile alpine vegetation.

The Long Trail cuts diagonally across the ridge to the west side and continues its southerly route. After hiking .7 miles from Taft Lodge you come to a sign for the Cliff Trail. Go right onto the unsigned, blue-blazed trail opposite the Cliff Trail. This is the Canyon North Extension.

Follow this trail as it leads west from the Long Trail. After approximately 250 feet the Subway Trail enters from the right. The Canyon North Extension swings left here. It is now marked with red paint splotches. Stay on it.

This soft, spongy path passes through thick stands of ever-greens. These trees shelter you from the winds which often buffet the mountain's west face.

Yellow blazes mark the entrance to the Little Subway on the left.

Cantilever Rock

This trail leads north and is an alternate approach to the Subway. Continue to follow the red blazes as they lead steeply downward. The path rises to cross over big boulders and passes under an overhanging ledge.

After winding left, the Canyon North Extension forks. A spur branches left down through a cave. A gentler path circles around and over the cave to the right, joining shortly with the left branch. From the narrow ledge just beyond the southern end of this cave, there are excellent views (look back) of Sunset Ridge.

Occasional breaks in the trees alongside the trail offer inter-mittent views to the west across Lake Champlain to the Adiron-dack Mountains. After a bit of easy rock scrambling, the Can-yon North Extension terminates at the Canyon North Trail after 1.3 miles from the beginning of the day's hike.

The Canyon North Trail (also red-blazed) enters from the left at this junction and swings south along the west side of the moun-tain. Follow it south. Short, young trees hide the trail and make the footing uncertain. Soon a "windowed" cave is reached

Mount Mansfield

on the left. Yellow blazes mark a steep ascent to the Long Trail above (but don't take it).

Squeeze yourself and your pack through the caves, crevices, and overhanging ledge. Watch carefully for the infrequent red blazes. At one point you approach a long stretch of ledge rising vertically at the left side of the trail. Look for the somewhat-hidden path as it makes a sharp turn opposite a red blaze near the beginning of the ledge.

The way passes over an assortment of rocks, roots, and ledge, making the going slow. The trail makes its only ascent, over loose rocks and small pieces of ledge, to its terminus (after 1.8 miles) at the blue-blazed Halfway House Trail.

Cross straight over the Halfway House Trail and continue south on the red-blazed Canyon Trail.

After a steep downward pitch the way passes through a deep crevice. Rock walls rise high above. At the far end, there is a low rock tunnel leading into the canyon. You must remove your pack and slide it through behind you as you edge through this low, caved area.

At the end of this passageway,

climb down the ladder to the canyon floor. The massive ledge walls lean outward to the right. Follow the trail as it tunnels down to still another level. It is again necessary to remove your pack and slither through the narrow opening.

The trail then emerges back onto the mountain's western slope. There are more narrow passages between giant boulders before the path passes over open ledge offering fine views to the west.

The Canyon Trail enters balsam and spruce woods and makes a steadily-steepening ascent to the crest of the ridge. The Lake View Trail leads southwest on the right just before the Canyon and Long Trails intersect at the Summit Station.

Pause to enjoy a grand view of the eastern horizon. The nearby coin-operated public telescope will bring everything even closer. Snacks may be purchased here during the summer months.

Continue following the Long Trail South for .3 miles. It leads over a boardwalk, through a wooded area, and onto the gravel road to the TV installation. Utilizing this road for a short distance, the trail bears right into the

woods and reaches the northern end of the Forehead Bypass just short of the TV station. Go left onto this white-blazed trail.

The Forehead Bypass begins a gentle descent over a soft dirt path. This ever-descending trail winds through open woods carpeted with a variety of green mosses. Clover-like wood sorrel flourishes here, while clumps of ferns raise their delicate fronds above the lower greenery.

The South Link leads left off the trail at the 3.1-mile point of today's hike. Continue right on the Forehead Bypass. Increasing its downward slope, the way descends over smooth-faced rocks. Roots traversing the path offer the only sure footing.

At the 4-mile point the Forehead Bypass reunites with the Long Trail. Go left onto the Long Trail and pass through the Needle's Eye. You then reach a clearing where a sign directs you left toward Taylor Lodge. Ignore this and look sharply right for the white "Butler Lodge" sign. Follow this trail down to the lodge.

This structure was constructed in 1933 by the Long Trail Patrol. From its picturesque setting you may enjoy a panorama

Mount Mansfield

of views. Butler Lodge faces southward down the chain of Green Mountains. To the west are the Champlain Valley and Adirondack mountains.

There is good water in a small brook just east of the lodge. Bunks and loft space can accommodate up to sixteen persons. This is a secure, cozy place to spend the night.

Fourth Day

You'll want to save this day as an extra in case of rain. If you are lucky enough to have five rain-free days, you might use it to explore some of Mount Mansfield's other trails. If so, we urge you to consult maps and descriptions of those trails before venturing out.

Fifth Day

Butler Lodge to Wampahoofus, The Forehead, Nose, and Vt. 108.

Class: IV
Vertical rise: 1,162 feet
Distance: 5.8 miles
Hiking time: 4¾ hours

Today's route takes you to several new points of interest. You'll see the famous Wampa-

White Birches

Mount Mansfield

hoofus. You'll also explore two final features of Mansfield's profile—the Forehead and Nose—and then enjoy far-reaching views to the east and southeast, before making your final descent to the mountain's base.

The Wampahoofus Trail is an exceptionally interesting one, as you will see. It begins at the right rear corner of Butler Lodge. The path leads north, and eventually east for .8 miles to the junction with the Long Trail near the Forehead.

Almost immediately after leaving the lodge, the Wampahoofus Trail makes a sharp swing to the left. Your way is blocked by a vertical ledge which must be scrambled over. At .1 miles the Rock Garden Trail branches off to the left. Continue straight here. Balsams fill the woods and sweeten the air with their fragrance.

The Wampahoofus Trail leads steeply upward. It twists and turns constantly as it climbs over and around huge boulders. Circling under overhanging ledge, the path becomes wet at times. Step carefully, especially when climbing on wet ledge.

Stands of short, scrawny white

birches edge the way as you climb toward massive outcroppings of ledge. The path seems to end abruptly at a high ledge. Climb to the right side and enter the long cave leading upward through the boulders. Overhead a small window through the rocks allows sun to enter the dim interior.

Ahead is an endless variety of rock shapes. Keep a close watch for that petrified creature who roamed the area many years ago—and may still. If you have not spotted the elusive Wampahoofus by the time the Maple Ridge Trail intersects at .6 miles, go back about 50 feet and look up. He lies with open jaws, directly overhead to the left.

The Wampahoofus was originally identified by Professor Roy O. Buchanan, founder of the Long Trail Patrol. According to Roy, the Sidehill Wampahoofus was a creature particularly well-adapted to travel on Vermont's mountains. With legs shorter on one side than the other, it was adept at grazing and pursuing prey on the steep slopes. Unfortunately, due to extensive inbreeding, all the females were born left-hand runners and all the males right-hand runners.

Thus, the males were unable to catch the females during mating season and no more Sidehill Wampahoofuses were born.

From the junction with the Maple Ridge Trail, the Wampahoofus turns sharply right and begins a steep ascent over smooth ledge. Natural indentations in the rock offer convenient footholds here. Scrub trees disappear, as the way continues steeply upward to its intersection with the Long Trail.

Continue on the Long Trail North .1 miles to the summit of the Forehead. A cairn-supported sign gives the elevation on this southernmost peak of Mount Mansfield as 3,940 feet. From here you can look out in all directions.

The Long Trail North continues its gradual way through alternately rocky and black, muddy areas. Trees become taller and offer shelter from the wind, as the path dips slightly and begins a gentle descent to the TV road. Just before this junction the Forehead Bypass enters from the right.

You reach the TV road after 1.2 miles of hiking from Butler Lodge. Look diagonally right

Mount Mansfield

across it. A sign marks the start of the Back Nose Trail. This brief path climbs steeply for .2 miles to the Nose and connects there with the Triangle Trail. It leads up over rock and ledge through low balsam and spruce. Winding out onto the open ledge and grassy area it passes the TV antennae and reaches the summit.

The elevation at the Nose is 4,062 feet. You can look back down upon the Forehead and up to the Lips, Chin, and Adam's Apple. Views in all directions.

Blue-painted triangles direct you eastward off the open ledge. The Triangle Trail extends .4 miles from the Nose to the Toll Road at the Octagon. It is a narrow trail which snakes over an endless succession of rocks, ledge, and roots. Footing is slippery, and precarious at times. Bushy balsam and spruce tug at your body as you wade through them.

The path leads to a small open lookout on the left. From here you have a spectacular view of the entire eastern side of Mount Mansfield—from the Chin to Vt. 108. Blue blazes are replaced by red ones as the path continues

its steep, ragged descent. The South Link joins the Triangle Trail just before the latter terminates at the Toll Road.

Directly across the road the Haselton Trail begins by following the Nose Dive Ski Trail down very steep slopes. You might want to sidestep a bit, to relieve the pressure on your knees. Staying inside the high wooden fences, go straight, then right, then left, and finally right once again. After passing a small hut on the trail's right side cut diagonally across to the left. Just past the last fence is a yellow sign to the Gondola. The Haselton Trail enters the woods to the left of this sign.

Watch for blue blazes behind the Gondola sign. The Haselton Trail might aptly be called the "water way." You see, hear, or walk through water almost all the way to the bottom.

The path swings steeply away from the ski trail and passes through wet, rocky areas. It leads over a small ski trail, crossing and paralleling trickling brooks in the process. After ½ mile, it traverses a larger ski trail and enters the woods again on the other side.

Several smaller brooks are crossed before the trail rock-hops over the South Stream. Continuing downward, you suddenly find yourself remaining elevated while streams drop away on both sides.

This hogback becomes soft underfoot as it passes between rows of waist-high evergreens. Needles carpet the path as it proceeds straight and flat along the ridge. Taller firs with needle-less limbs are passed before the younger, bushier ones take over again. By this time the streams have become faint rumbles far below.

Returning to its winding ways, the Haselton Trail begins a long, moderate-to-steep descent through thick woods. The path is soft and spongy underfoot. At the 3.3-mile point on this last day's hike it leads out onto a ski service road and follows it down to the Gondola Parking Area.

From here it is a short walk to Route 108 and a little over two miles back to your car.

Mount Mansfield